VOGUE® KNITTING
The Ultimate Sock Book

history   technique   design

the editors of Vogue Knitting Magazine

VOGUE® KNITTING

The Ultimate Sock Book

history   technique   design

the editors of Vogue Knitting Magazine

sixth&spring books

Sixth&Spring Books
233 Spring Street
New York, New York 10013

Editorial Director
Elaine Silverstein

Book Division Manager
Erica Smith

Associate Editor
Amanda Keiser

Art Director
Chi Ling Moy

Associate Art Director
Sheena T. Paul

Graphic Designer
Michael Yong

Editors
Adina Klein
Carla Scott

Contributors
Cathy Carron
Jean Lienhauser
Eve Ng
Michelle Wiener

Technical Editors
Eve Ng
Lisa Buccellato

Copy Editors
Marjorie Anderson
Kristina Sigler

Yarn Editor
Tanis Gray

Fashion Director
Misty Gunn

Bookings Editor
Rachael Stein

Production Associate
Sarah Baar

◼

Vice President, Publisher
Trisha Malcolm

Production Manager
David Joinnides

Creative Director
Joe Vior

President
Art Joinnides

Photo Credits :
Rose Callahan: Cover, pp. 5, 6, 7, 17 (middle), 42 (bottom), 142, 145, 162, 166.

Paul Amato for LVARepresents.com: pp. 2, 17 (top), 24, 40 (2nd from top), 41 (top), 43, 44, 45
(top and bottom), 54, 76, 78, 79, 99, 104, 107, 109, 110, 112, 113, 117, 122, 130, 133, 137, 138, 146,
154, 157.

Marcus Tullis: pp. 16, 17 (bottom), 35, 37, 38, 39, 40 (top), 40 (bottom), 41 (bottom), 42 (top),
49, 80, 82, 84, 86, 87, 88, 92, 96, 98, 118, 121, 126, 150, 158, 161.

Cathy Carron: pp. 8, 15, 19-23.

Jack Deutsch: pp. 56-75.

Eye[4]Media/Bobb Connors: pp. 11 (bottom), 101.

V&A Images/Victoria and Albert Museum: p.11 (top).

First Edition
3 5 7 9 10 8 6 4 2
Manufactured in China

Library of Congress Control Number: 2007920926
ISBN: 1-933027-19-3
ISBN-13: 978-1-933027-19-7

Contents

Introduction

I have a confession to make: until a few years ago, I was a member of the non-sock-knitting population. Sure, I knew how to make a sock; I just chose not to.

Then, seemingly overnight, sock knitters were everywhere: in cafes, at doctors' offices, on the subway. From the way these acolytes talked, sock knitting was more than the next knitting fad—it was a transcendental experience. So one day I took some leftover yarn from a baby sweater and decided to see what all the fuss was about.

What I found is that sock knitting is the distillation of knitting at its finest. It is a combination of meditative, mindless knitting and technically accomplished craft. Socks can be as basic or as challenging as the knitter wants to make them: you can knit a simple tube sock out of self-striping yarn or a technically advanced toe-up sock with colorwork or cables. What's more, socks can easily be modified for a perfect fit, and the finished project works with any body type. I find constructing a three-dimensional object with nothing more than string and needles a magical, transformative act.

Knit a sock and you're instantly connected to a tradition that spans continents and centuries. Long before there were knitwear designers or printed books, or even a common language in which to convey knitting instructions, people all around the world were creating socks, determining the geometry of a hand-knit heel, figuring calf-shaping decreases, crafting works of art out of the fiber, stitches and patterns endemic to their geographic location and culture. Once you've glimpsed the infinite possibilities of sock knitting, it's impossible to think of this craft as anything less than poetry.

I am proud to introduce our **Vogue Knitting Ultimate Sock Book**. Inside, knitters new to the art will be guided step by step through the wonders of sock construction. Knitters already initiated into the glory of socks will find historical background on socks from all over the world and guidelines for designing socks of their own. Interspersed throughout each chapter are patterns from highly talented designers to provide you with fresh challenges and inspiration. Knitters of all skill levels will find something within these pages to fascinate, teach or pique their curiosity.

Adina Klein
Editor in Chief, **Vogue Knitting**

Chapter 1
History of Sock Knitting

Whether you are brand-new to sock knitting or a voracious practitioner, welcome to your place in knitting history. The history of sock knitting is essentially the history of all knitting as we know it: socks were among the first knitted garments. Found during archaeological digs in Egypt and surrounding countries, the earliest socks were brilliant, elaborate pieces with bands of colorwork, the cotton fiber dyed with plants and berries. Some early socks found in the Near East incorporate the early Arabic word for Allah. The first knitters got it right: hand-knit socks are holy objects.

Early History

The history of socks starts as early as c. 700 B.C., when people covered their legs and feet with animal hides, as the Greek poet Hesiod describes in "Works and Days": "And on your feet bind boots of the hide of the slaughtered ox, fitting them closely, when you have cushioned their insides with felt." "Felt" here means something similar to the way knitters understand the word today—matted animal hair. Ancient Roman men wore *fasciae* (sing. *fascia*), strips of fabric made from cloth or leather to cover their shins and legs and often their feet as well. Soldiers wore fasciae for protection in battle, older men and women to keep warm. Milton Grass tells us in *A History of Hosiery* that men who wore fasciae when not in the military were considered weak. However, by the first century A.D., attitudes toward footwear had changed, and the fascia was considered a sign of wealth and culture—for men, at least. It was around this time that fasciae gave way to *udones*, slippers of animal fur or felt that were pulled on rather than wrapped.

The practice of wearing socks traveled with the Romans to England, proof of which was discovered during an excavation at Vindolanda, a settlement along Hadrian's Wall. There, archaeologists unearthed a small child's cloth bootie as well as a wooden tablet inscribed with a letter to a Roman soldier indicating that the writer had sent a package of socks and sandals. By the mid fifth century, Saxon clothing included the *socque*, a short stocking of leather or cloth worn with knee-length trousers, and leg bindings called *scanc-beorg*. Similar dress appeared in France, with pants becoming longer and tighter below the knee, until the twelfth century when the lower leg earned a separate covering. Known as *chausses* in French and *hose* in English, these stockings of linen or wool sometimes had no feet, sometimes had stirrups that fit under the feet and sometimes had whole feet. Eventually hose replaced bindings, and by the fourteenth century, they had become more decorative, often striped in different colors and with toes stuffed with wool or linen to make them more pronounced, as was the fashion. The instep could also be embroidered or jeweled—a precursor to clocks, described later in this chapter.

Fragments of what look like knitted socks were found at the site of Dura-Europos, a city in what is now modern-day Syria, founded after the death of Alexander the Great. The city, once a thriving trading center, was obliterated by Persian troops in 256 A.D., so the sock fragments must predate that time. They are commonly considered the oldest examples of knitting, though there is some dispute over the exact technique used to create the fabric. The Victoria and Albert Museum in London houses a remarkably well-preserved pair of Coptic (Egyptian) socks dating from the third to fifth centuries. The socks are bright red and have a split toe, indicating that they were worn with sandals. They have a gorgeous, complex design worthy of knitting. But they are not knitted.

Instead, the socks were created by a method called *nalbinding* (also spelled *naalebinding* and *nålbinding*, pronounced NAWL-bin-ding), which uses a single needle and short lengths of yarn. Unlike knitting or crochet, which never use the tail end of the working yarn, nalbinding requires one to pull the full length of yarn through one or more loops. The resulting fabric resembles knitting and is very dense and sturdy, so it provides good protection and warmth for feet. It is not particularly elastic, however, nor is nalbinding an efficient method of creating fabric, both important factors when it comes to creating a protective covering for the feet.

The Emergence of Knitting

Richard Rutt, in *A History of Hand Knitting*, estimates that knitting replaced nalbinding as a preferred method of creating fabric between the sixth and thirteenth centuries. The earliest true knitted pieces, made with two needles pulling loops out of other loops, were liturgical gloves worn by European bishops, dating from no earlier than the seventh century. In Italy during the fourteenth century, several painters portrayed the Virgin Mary knitting (in the round, with four or five needles). And in England, the verb "to knit" entered the vernacular some time in the fifteenth century. The earliest known knitted socks, discovered in the Middle East, also fall within this time period. They are described at the beginning of this chapter: worked toe up, with banded patterns incorporating the word Allah in Kufic script. Archaeologists date the socks from between the thirteenth and sixteenth centuries, and the appearance of knitted socks in different geographical locations at roughly the same time indicates that knitting traveled between the Middle East and Continental Europe, eventually migrating north to England.

Historians have suggested several ways that the skill could have spread. The Muslim expansion of 710 A.D. probably brought knitting to Spain, a reasonable theory because Spain led Europe in the production of finely knitted silk stockings. Trade routes via land and sea would also have influenced the distribution of materials and skills to other countries. And let's not overlook the role the

Crusades might have played, though the propagation of knitting will most likely remain an overlooked event in history textbooks.

By the start of the sixteenth century, folks all around Europe were knitting socks. The fiber content varied depending on economic status: royalty and aristocracy were decked out in Spanish or Italian silk stockings crafted on slender metal needles, while commoners wore coarse hose made from wool they spun themselves and knit on larger needles. Eventually there was a leveling of fiber and class, as the metalworking techniques that were developed in Mediterranean countries made their way to England, and woolen stockings knit on finer needles became the norm for the masses.

It is possible, as Rutt demonstrates, to trace the history of British socks through British royal history. Henry VIII was the first British monarch to don a pair of hand-knitted stockings, silk as befit a king. His successor, Edward VI, received Spanish silk stockings as a gift from Sir Thomas Gresham, a financier working for the king. (Sir Thomas would continue to work for Queen Elizabeth and would also bestow socks upon her.) There is some speculation that Mary Queen of Scots learned to knit herself, but as there is no mention of any other royal personage knitting, this seems unlikely. We do know is that Mary wore knitted socks to her execution in 1586, of "worsted, coloured watchett [blue], clocked with silver and edged at the tops with silver."

Clocks, or *clox*, were decorative flourishes found on socks of this period. The term's etymology is

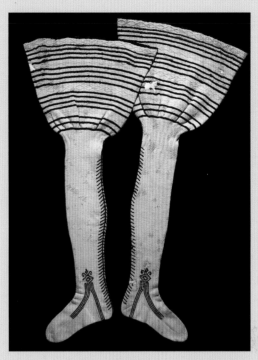

An Englishman's elaborate stockings from the seventeenth century have flared tops to fit over boots as well as beautifully embroidered clocks.

A modern recreation of Eleanora of Toledo's red silk stockings by Margaret Stove. You can knit these beautiful and historic stockings using the pattern on page 101.

vague; one theory suggests the name comes from the early designs' resemblance to the hands or pendulum of a timepiece. Clocks were fashioned on both sides of the ankle, either by embroidery or with a combination of knit and purl stitches. They were intended to make this part of the sock more durable, but then as now, fashion was not sacrificed for function. As the stocking trade burgeoned and mass production took over, machine-made socks were sent to cottagers to hand-sew the clocks. The job was called "chevening" because the adornments resembled a chevron pattern.

Many gorgeous, highly ornamented pairs of stockings were knit for lucky royals during the Renaissance. Eleanora of Toledo, wife of Cosimo de Medici, grand duke of Tuscany, owned one of the most stunning pairs. Eleanora died in 1562; the stockings were unearthed from her tomb. They were made of crimson-dyed silk, with an elegant eyelet diamond cuff bordered by a zigzag purl pattern, on top of a leg featuring vertical panels of moss stitch and a variation of garter stitch. (Margaret Stove recreated these socks for the modern knitter, and the pattern appears on page 101.) The stockings worn by Gustavus Adolphus, king of Sweden from 1611 to 1632, at his coronation were 26 inches long, knit in white silk at a gauge of 25 stitches and 32 rows to the inch. (A little math reveals that at least 250 stitches were cast on for each sock.)

It would be possible to produce a laundry list of stockings worn by the kings and queens of Europe, but it wouldn't be quite as interesting as the many stories about Queen Elizabeth I and her footwear. Chronicler Edmund Howes records that, in 1560, the queen received her first pair of silk stockings from her silk woman, Mistress Montague, and was so taken with them that she pronounced, "Henceforth I will wear no more cloth stockings." Records show that the following New Year, she received three pairs of silk stockings as gifts. A man named William Lee invented a knitting frame to use with wool and presented it to the queen in application for a patent, which she refused. An article published at the turn of the twentieth century quotes a letter purportedly written by Elizabeth explaining her refusal: "Had Mr. Lee made a machine that would have made silk stockings, I should, I think, have been somewhat justified in granting him a patent for that monoply [sic], which would have effected [sic] only a small number of my subjects." But wool knitting was the source of income for too many people, and replacing hand-knitters with a machine would have destroyed their livelihood.

For all her love of silk, records show that Elizabeth began wearing knitted wool stockings in 1577. And did William Lee ever have an audience with the Queen? We don't know. In any case, Lee never did receive an English patent for his knitting frame, even after designing one for silk yarn, and he wound up seeking his fortune in France. But regardless of the wisdom—or lack of it—evinced by Elizabeth's refusal of the patent, she certainly appreciated how special knit stockings were. She was a very smart queen.

The English Sock Industry

By the end of the sixteenth century, hand-knitted stockings were a burgeoning export industry throughout Europe. Brightly colored stockings often became objects of ridicule (think of Malvolio's yellow stockings in Shakespeare's *Twelfth Night*), their wearers perceived as dandies, but the act of knitting was considered a respectable domestic activity, one that conferred economic advantages as well. People knit socks for themselves and for their families, but demand was so high that knitting provided many families with a supplemental income. Socks were a portable project, meaning knitters could produce them while engaged in other household or farming chores. According to estimates, 200,000 people in Great Britain were knitting socks by the end of the sixteenth century, producing twenty million pairs a year.

The significant demand for hand-knit socks may be a key reason why it is a sock for which the first known English printed pattern was published in 1655, in a small volume meant for household use (perhaps we might think of it as a precursor to *Good Housekeeping*). As Rutt describes, the pattern, called "The order how to knit a hose," is incredibly difficult for modern eyes to read. Its punctuation and spelling are inconsistent (grammar and syntax would not be standardized for another century at least), and the entire pattern is all one sentence—three pages long!

The hand-knit sock's fame led to a backlash. In 1583, Philip Stubbs, a cantankerous pamphleteer, published "The Anatomie of Abuses," a diatribe on everything, including the "impudent insolency and shameful outrage" of the stocking fad: "…every one, almost, though otherwise very poor, having scarcely forty shillings of wages by the year, will not stick to have two or three pair of these silk nether-stocks, or else of the finest yarn that can be got, though the price of them be a royal…. The time hath been when one might have clothed all his body well from top to toe for less than a pair of these nether-socks will cost." Women were singled out as the worst offenders, for wearing stockings "of all kinds of changeable colors" without shame.

The popularity of knitting and the demand for hand-knit goods led to the establishment of knitting schools, the first one in York in 1588. The schools taught skills to the poor, particularly children, to give them a means of financial support and keep them out of trouble.

These schools would continue long after knitting frames became the chief method of producing socks, largely due to the tempering effect knitting was believed to have. The famous philanthropist and writer Hannah More taught knitting and spinning, connecting them in her writings to virtue and prudence. The idea that knitting was a good way to keep hands safely busy made its way to the American Colonies.

In North America

The British put in place strict exporting rules, including one that forbade the shipment of knitting frames to the Colonies. Parliament further tightened the reins in 1699 with the Woolen Act, which outlawed the export of wool and wool products from the Colonies to anywhere else. The Colonists duly ignored these laws, but with materials scarce, they needed to fend for themselves and so made do with cloth or hand-knit socks. Few existing texts record who knit and when, but one delightful relic survives in the form of a teenage girl's diary, in which she records how much she knit on a stocking per day: "Knit two inches...knit a long piece...finish'd the foot by candlelight." While today's recreational knitters sometimes see one finished sock as cause for rejoicing, and dread having to start all over on the second, Colonial knitters didn't have the luxury of suffering the proverbial Second Sock Syndrome. If a sock languished in the workbasket, someone went without.

Much of the history of American sock knitting is tangled up in war. Starting with the Revolutionary War, women knit socks for soldiers. But unlike later wars, during the Revolutionary War, women went straight to the front to bring socks and other needed items to the fighting men. The future first First Lady was a prime organizer of the knitting effort and always seemed to have a sock in progress. Martha Washington is remembered to have been a galvanizing force for both soldiers and ladies, connecting knitting with independence and American spirit in a way that should send shivers down even the most jaded spine: "American ladies should be patterns of industry to their countrywomen, because the separation from the mother country will dry up resources whence many of our conflicts have been derived," one woman recalls Martha Washington saying. "We must become independent by our determination to do without what we cannot ourselves make. Whilst our husbands and brothers are examples of patriotism, we must be patterns of industry."

Fans of Louisa May Alcott may remember the continual knitting references in *Little Women*, beginning with the first chapter, in which Jo March is knitting a "blue army sock" for a Union soldier. Women organized in droves, unprompted and unsolicited by the government, to knit socks for soldiers fighting the Civil War—on both sides. While machine-made socks were readily available by this time, soldiers preferred the hand-knit socks because they were thicker, warmer and more durable. The Northern knitters, like their soldiers, had more resources at their disposal than did their Southern counterparts. It's hard not to admire the resolve and ingenuity of the women of the war-weary South, who unraveled previously knitted items to obtain wool for socks.

By World War I the demand was so great that the sock effort switched to machine production, but women still knit socks to send off to France. Veterans of the Civil War—soldiers and knitters alike—joined the new war effort, and even Governor George W. P. Hunt of Arizona unabashedly knit socks for American troops. Thanks in large part to the organizational skills and volunteer efforts of the Red Cross, everyone across the country was "knitting for Sammie." Other groups remained autonomous in their knitting drive, like the Self-Improvement Club of Seattle, which focused its energy on knitting socks for soldiers of color, which they packaged along with other comfort items and letters of support. By the war's end, the knitting drive had grown to include women and children refugees. World War II saw similar proceedings; though the 1930s saw a slight decline in hand knitting, the relief knitting effort sparked its comeback. (See the photo essay on pages 18–23.)

Richard Rutt states that hand-knit socks have all but disappeared, reasoning, "Stockings were always dull work. Today's knitter expects more pleasure from the craft." While this may have been the case when his book was published in 1987, the landscape of knitting has certainly changed, and socks have returned to their former prominence. But it is also true that there were moments in the past when sock knitting fulfilled more than a basic clothing need. At the end of the nineteenth century, scores of American women shed their ankle-length dresses in favor of bloomers, which accommodated the new sport of bicycling. Bicycling, in fact, required a whole new wardrobe—if not bloomers, then shorter skirts that wouldn't catch on the spokes. The new dress combined with the new sport in turn required—yes, new socks. Fancy socks. Fancy socks with patterns that would look good against the wheel, peeking out of the top of

Women have always participated in war efforts by knitting socks for soldiers.

ladies' cycling boots. Knitted bicycling socks resembled leggings with a foot stirrup, with the leg and foot sections knit in plain, dull colors, while the cuff sported fancy stitches and multicolor designs.

The rage for hand-knit socks resurfaced in the 1940s and '50s with the growing popularity of argyle patterns. Argyle socks were marketed to young female knitters as a tried-and-true way of securing a mate. Wow him with a pair of hand-knitted argyle socks. In the 1950s, everyone had a pair of argyle socks on the needles (some of them still do).

The pattern for these classic men's argyle socks, designed by Shirley Paden, is on page 158.

Today and Beyond

As it was in the 1950s, it's true that today, no one *needs* hand-knit socks. It is far more economical in terms of both time and money to buy socks—and the market is saturated with crazy, colorful, patterned ones. While some people knit socks for charity projects, they aren't as quick a knit as hats or even mittens or as automatic as a garter-stitch blanket. So why knit socks? What's the appeal?

Ask any sock knitter and you won't get just answers. You'll get poetry. Candace Eisner Strick calls sock knitting "a way of life." For Charlene Schurch, socks are "superlative knitting. I have great admiration for those knitters who figured out the heel and shared it with the rest of us." "The truth about socks," writes Stephanie Pearl-McPhee, "is that they're humble and beautiful and noble, and in their lowness they're the highest form of art." Nancy Bush likens the act of knitting a sock to a dance. Others liken the formation of a sock to the creation of sculpture.

More than any other knitted garment, creating a sock is a magical experience. "The geography of the foot makes sock-knitting physically pleasurable, like a joyride steered with needles in hand," says Cat Bordhi, "from the thrill of expanding and then contracting over the swell of the heel, to decreasing down the slope of the instep, and finally the satisfaction of closure at the toe." That a sock is both small and portable and a project that requires a bit of brain power means it's just the thing to maintain sanity while waiting for a doctor's appointment, commuting by train, or attending a meeting or lecture.

The basic sock pattern is the same today as it was 500 years ago. Then, as now, there were both a variety of fibers as well as several different techniques to choose from: knit from the cuff down or from the toe up, with numerous different styles of heels and toes. These methods were specific to a geographic location and custom in the past, and the wealth of options knitters have today is the result of years of travel, research and design—and another reason why sock knitting will never get boring. Tired of the same old Dutch heel? Try a Welsh or French one. Make a sock with a star-point toe. To many sock knitters, the use of four or five double-point needles holds enormous value, because of the technique's connection with the past. It is entirely possible to imagine oneself manipulating the same stitches in the same way as women did in the seventeenth century. To get the full historical fix, it's now possible to recreate as many sock patterns of the past as a knitter wants, thanks to sock-knitting ethnographers such as Priscilla Gibson-Roberts and Nancy Bush.

For other knitters, innovation is the key. Feeling the connection to history remains a part of the joy, but new yarns and new technology—not to mention a few genius moments—allow for faster, stronger (though maybe not quite bionic) socks. Nancy Bush reminds us that, to a knitter of the nineteenth century, the "slip, slip, knit" of heel-turning would have been an innovation, so it's not hard to imagine a sock knitter of centuries past marveling at the engineering of circular needles. Knitters who find all those double-pointed needles cumbersome and awkward will indeed find that "socks soar" with Cat Bordhi's book detailing how to knit socks on two circular needles (see Patterns). And if two is too many, there's the "Magic Loop" method, which uses one circular needle with a 40" flexible cable.

For every knitter, there is a sock pattern tailored for her or his specific knitting abilities and needs. So in a way, this book has been many centuries in the making.

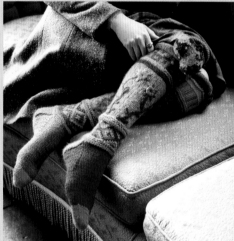

Contemporary socks by (top to bottom) Meg Swansen, Kristin Nicholas and Priscilla Gibson-Roberts interpret classic designs and traditions in fresh new ways. The patterns are at the end of this book.

Socks in Wartime

By Cathy Carron

Socks have been hand knit for soldiers and armies for hundreds of years. One of the earliest recorded instances took place in England during Europe's Seven Years' War (1756–1763). The most spectacular display ever of wartime knitting occurred during the so-called Great War—World War I. During this war, women's changing roles in Western society intersected with the government's frequent calls for massive amounts of war supplies. It was a meeting of willingness and need: women wanted to be a part of the war effort, but because their role was limited, they devised their own ways to participate, which included making bandages, collecting recyclable materials, preparing care packages for the soldiers, raising produce and, of course, knitting.

Women and men in both Axis and Allied countries knitted for their troops, but Great Britain dominated the effort, because it was the country that actively controlled and eventually came to monopolize the world's wool supply. Recognizing the strategic importance of wool, early in the war the British government struck a deal with the wool-producing Commonwealth countries, primarily Australia and New Zealand, to purchase their entire wool clips for the duration of the war. This act of economic warfare ensured that Great Britain and the Allies would have enough wool for uniforms and the enemy Axis powers would not. With no substitute fibers available, Great Britain and eventually the United States listed wool as one of the top ten strategic materials of the war.

War knitting took hold in Great Britain at the cannons' first roar. American expatriates in London began to urge women stateside to take up their needles as well, which they did, but serious effort on the American side didn't really begin until the United States declared war in April 1917. Surprisingly, American governmental officials tried to thwart the women's efforts, voicing concern about the country's limited wool supply and hinting at male chauvinism. Only after General Pershing's request, late in the summer of 1917, that his troops be provided with two million sets of hand-knitted wear—vest, scarf and socks—did the knitting craze really start in the United States. Record low temperatures in Europe over the two previous winters prompted this requisition. Over the next nineteen months, until the war ended, American women made over fourteen million hand-knitted articles for the troops. This was a valiant and poignant endeavor by hundreds of thousands of women, and a few good men. To them, clicking their knitting needles was the same as wielding the arms they were forbidden to bear.

Active Service

In Britain during World War I, knitting needles were women's weapons and knitting was commonly equated with "fighting the battle" and "a call to arms." It was one of the few ways women could participate in the war effort, and more women knitted during this period than did any other single war-related activity.

We all are trying to do our bit: Knitting Sweaters, Socks and Helmets.

This American postcard relies on patriotic imagery to encourage women to "do their bit" for the World War I effort.

Für Unsre Feldgrauen (For Our Soldiers)

This German card is extremely rare. German women began to knit at the outset of the war but found it increasingly difficult to procure wool as time went on. During World War I wool was a strategic material and was a highly valued commodity for lack of substitutes and a shortage of indigenous supplies. As the war progressed German women hardly knit at all, and when they did it was necessary to unwind other garments and reuse the wool.

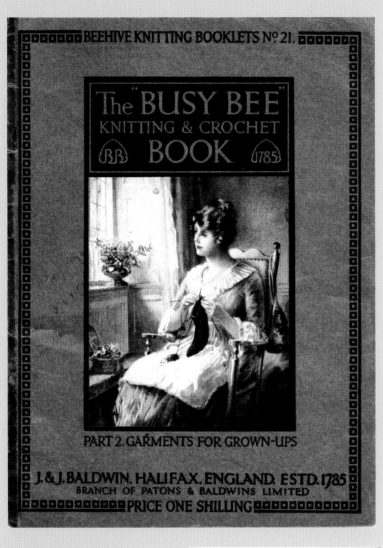

Busy Bee Cover and Sock Pattern, World War I

British women have had a long history of knitting socks for the military and were quick to take up their needles, or as they say "pins," again with the onset of World War I, the period in which this pattern book was published. All sorts of patterns were offered up until the British Red Cross stepped in to standardize design and production.

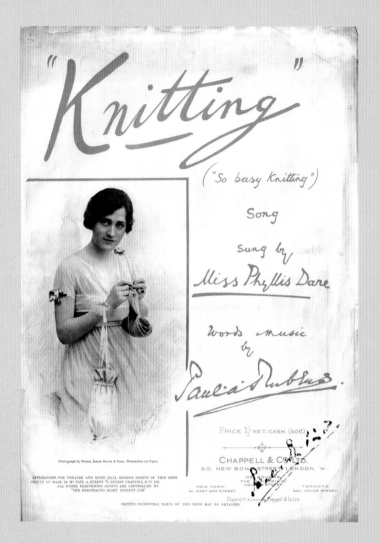

Sheet Music

Knitting for the soldiers found expression is literature, poetry and music throughout the two world wars, but this expression flourished most strongly during World War I. Poetry contests resulted in hundreds of poems, and over two dozen songs were written, including "Knitting, So Busy Knitting" (1915) by Paul A. Rubens. During World War II, songs like "A Soldier's Socks" recounted the "20,000 little stitches, go to make a soldier's sock," but it was Glenn Miller's song "Knit One, Purl Two" that became the knitting music sensation of the war.

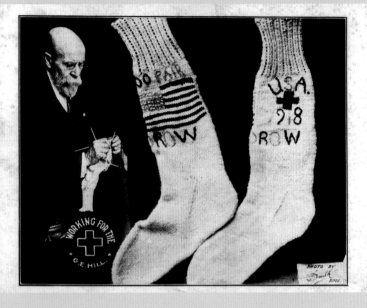

A PAIR
OF SOCKS
FOR
PRESIDENT
WILSON,
KNIT BY
GEO. E. HILL
104
CENTER ST.,
DAYTON, O.

A0649

Post Card

2 CENT
STAMP
HERE

Faithful Red Cross Worker

That others may be influenced to take up the Red Cross work, we are presenting you with this card, showing George E. Hill at work knitting. This is his one hundredth pair of socks and this pair is to be presented to **President Wilson.** Mr. Hill does his knitting from 3 a. m. to 7 a. m. and also Sundays, completing a pair each Sunday.

SMITH BROS., Photographers,
18 E. Fourth St., Dayton, O.

(OVER)

American Red Cross Propaganda

Men did their bit, too: this propaganda card displays the work of a "faithful Red Cross worker" who completed a pair of socks each week and presented this ceremonial pair to President Wilson.

Chapter 2
Basic Techniques

Sock knitting requires only a few basic knitting skills: casting

on, knitting in the round, decreasing, working short rows,

picking up stitches, binding off and seamless joining (often

called grafting or Kitchener stitch). There's actually less

shaping involved in making a sock than in making a basic

sweater with set-in sleeves—and there's certainly much less

finishing. In fact, once you've completed a sock, the only thing

left to do is weave in the yarn ends, and unless you've used

more than one yarn color, there are only two ends.

Simplicity indeed!

This chapter explains and illustrates all these basic techniques.

In Chapter 3, we show you how to put them together to make

socks using the two most common techniques: working from

the top, or cuff, down, and working from the toe up.

Casting On

FOR TOP-DOWN SOCKS

There are many ways to cast on for knitting, but when making top-down socks, choose a method that gives a firm but stretchy edge. We've shown two good choices here: the standard long-tail cast-on and the cable cast-on. Before casting on, place a slipknot on the needle (see Appendix). Then proceed to the cast-on method you have chosen. If you are going to be working in the round with four or five needles, cast the stitches onto one needle, then divide them on three or four needles before working the first row.

Long-Tail Cast-On This method gives a firm but stretchy edge, so it is a good one for socks. First make a slipknot on the needle, leaving a long yarn end. For socks, figure on about ½" for each stitch, plus 8" for use in finishing later. Hold the needle in the right hand.

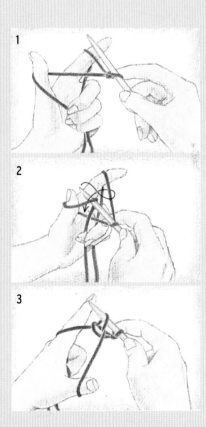

Step 1: Bring the yarn tail end around the left thumb from front to back; then wrap the yarn from the ball over the left index finger. Hold the ends firmly in your palm.

Step 2: Insert the right needle upward in the thumb loop. With the needle tip, draw the yarn from the ball through the loop to form a stitch.

Step 3: Remove your thumb from the loop and tighten the loop on the needle. It should be firm, but not tight, and should slide easily along the needle.

Repeat Steps 1 through 3 for each stitch to be cast on.

Cable Cast-On This method is good for socks, because it gives a sturdy and elastic edge. It makes a nice start for ribbing.

Step 1: Make a slipknot on a needle, leaving only an 8" to 10" yarn end.

Insert the right needle from front to back into the stitch on left needle.

Wrap the yarn around the right needle as if to knit.

Step 2: Draw the yarn through the first stitch, making a new stitch, but do not drop the first stitch from the left needle. Slip the new stitch to the left needle and remove the right needle from stitch. You now have two stitches, counting the slipknot as a stitch.

Step 3: Insert the right needle between the two stitches on the left needle.

Step 4: Wrap the yarn around the right needle as if to knit, and draw the yarn through to make a new stitch.

Step 5: Place the new stitch on the left needle.

Repeat Steps 3 through 5 for each stitch to be cast on, always inserting the right needle between the last two stitches on the left needle.

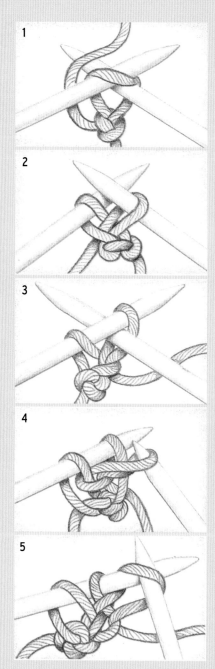

FOR TOE-UP SOCKS

When making toe-up socks, use a provisional cast-on. Cast on using waste yarn, and remove the cast-on row after you have completed the toe. This allows you to begin working in the round with the correct number of live stitches.

Crochet Cast-On The simplest provisional cast-on is an open-chain, or crochet cast-on. Begin by crocheting a foundation chain. Your chain should be several stitches longer than the number of stitches to be cast on.

Make a Foundation Chain

Step 1: Start by making a slipknot and positioning it near the end of the hook. Wrap the working yarn (the yarn attached to the ball or skein) around the hook as shown. Wrapping the yarn in this way is called a yarn over (yo).

Step 2: Draw the yarn through the loop on the hook by catching it with the hook and pulling towards you.

Step 3: One chain stitch is complete. Repeat from Step 1 to make as many chains as required.

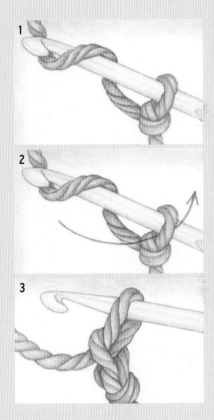

To use the crochet chain as the foundation for the first row of knitting, pick up one stitch in the back loop of each chain, using main-color yarn. Once you have completed your toe or heel, carefully remove the crochet chain and place the resulting live stitches on a needle.

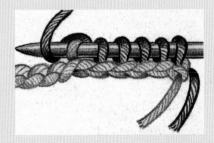

With main-color yarn, pick up one stitch in the back loop of each chain.

Working in the Round

To avoid the need for seams, most socks are worked in the round on a set of four or five double-pointed needles, although some knitters prefer to use one or two circular needles (see Flow Motion Socks, page 113). When working with double-pointed needles, divide the stitches evenly among three or four needles; use the remaining needle as your working needle. It is slightly easier to knit top-down socks using a set of five needles. To work the heel flap on a top-down sock, you use exactly half the stitches. Therefore, if you begin the sock with the stitches divided evenly on four needles, you simply hold two needles at the back and combine the stitches from the other two needles onto a single needle for the heel.

To use four needles instead of five, put one-half of the total number of stitches on one of the working needles and one-quarter of the stitches on each of the two other needles.

Here are some tips for avoiding "ladders" caused by uneven tension when working with double-pointed needles:
• If you are knitting a stitch pattern that combines knit and purl stitches, such as a ribbing, make the join between needles fall at a place where there are adjacent knit and purl stitches.
• As you work the stitches on each needle, hold the point of the previous needle *below* the working needle.
• Do not pull the yarn tight as you work the first stitch on each needle. Instead, give an extra, gentle tug on the yarn as you work the second stitch on each needle. You should actually see the previous needle snug right up against the working needle. This will avoid a gap between the stitches on the two needles.

Casting On and Knitting With Double-Pointed Needles

Cast on with three needles.

Step 1: Cast on the required number of stitches on the first needle, plus one extra. Slip this extra stitch to the next needle as shown. Continue in this way, casting on the required number of stitches on the last needle.

Step 2: Arrange the needles as shown, with the cast-on edge facing the center of the triangle (or square).

Step 3: Place a stitch marker after the last cast-on stitch. With the free needle, knit the first cast-on stitch, pulling the yarn tightly. Continue knitting in rounds, slipping the marker before beginning each round.

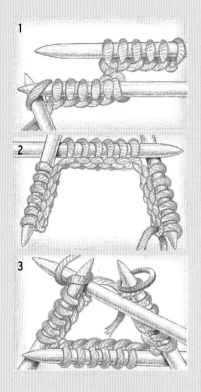

Here are two tips for creating a neat joining on the first round:
• Work the first few stitches with both the working yarn and the cast-on tail held together.
• When casting on, cast on one extra stitch. Slip this stitch to the first needle. On the first round of knitting, work it together with the first cast-on stitch.

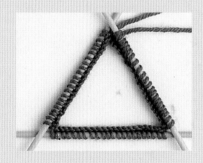

Decreasing

Socks are shaped by decreasing (reducing the number of stitches). It is important to use balanced decreases. This means that the decreases on the left half of your work slant to the right, and those on the right half of your work slant to the left.

Right-slanting decrease

Knitting (or purling) two stitches together causes the work to slant to the right on the knit side of a piece. This technique is abbreviated k2tog (or p2tog).

K2tog: Insert right needle knitwise through both of the next two stitches on the left needle, and knit them off together. You have decreased one stitch.

P2tog: Insert right needle purlwise through both of the next two sts on the left needle, and purl them off together. You have decreased one stitch.

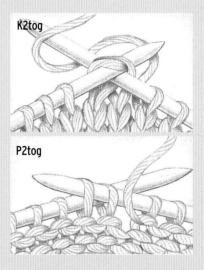

Left-slanting decrease

This method causes the work to slant to the left on the knit side of a piece. The technique is abbreviated ssk (slip, slip, knit, or slip 1, slip 1, k2tog).

Ssk

Step 1: Slip the next two stitches from the left needle to the right needle one at a time, inserting the right needle tip knitwise.

Step 2: Insert the left needle into the fronts of the two slipped stitches and knit them off together as one.

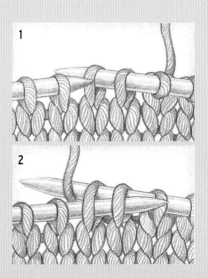

Working Short Rows

Short rows are partial rows of knitting used to shape curved sections, such as toes and heels. Working the toes and heels of toe-up socks requires two special, but easy techniques: wrap and turn and working (or picking up) the wraps. The heels of top-down socks use a streamlined technique that does not require wrapping and working the wraps (the technique for making a simple short-row heel is in Chapter 3).

Step 1: To prevent holes in the piece and create a smooth transition, wrap a knit stitch as follows: with the yarn in back, slip the next stitch purlwise.

Step 2: Move the yarn between the needles to the front of the work.

Step 3: Slip the same stitch back to the left needle. Turn the work, bringing the yarn to the purl side between the needles. One stitch is wrapped.

Step 4: When you have completed all the short rows, you must hide (pick up) the wraps. Work to just before the wrapped stitch. Insert the right needle under the wrap and knitwise into the wrapped stitch. Knit them together.

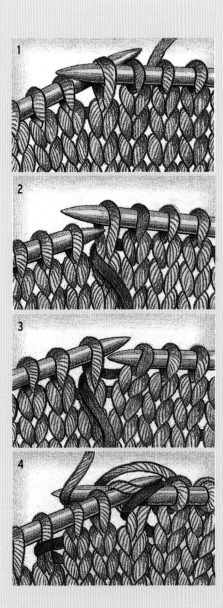

FRONT LOOP, BACK LOOP

When instructions say to work in the front or back loop of a stitch, you need to know what this means. Whether you are knitting or purling, the front loop always means the loop closer to you; the back loop always means the loop farther away from you.

SLIPPING STITCHES

Stitches can be slipped either knitwise, with the right needle inserted as if to knit, or purlwise, with the right needle inserted as if to purl. The slipped stitches are moved from one needle to the other without being worked.

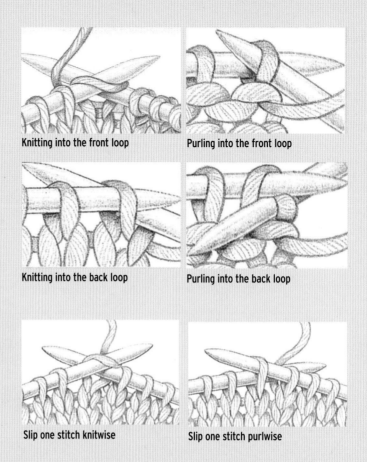

Knitting into the front loop

Purling into the front loop

Knitting into the back loop

Purling into the back loop

Slip one stitch knitwise

Slip one stitch purlwise

Picking Up Stitches

When working a gusset on a top-down sock, you will usually need to pick up stitches along the sides of the rows forming the heel flap. Most instructions for knitting heel flaps tell you to slip the first stitch of each row. This gives you a neat chain of stitches down both sides of the flap, allowing you to pick up one stitch in each link of the chain. To avoid a hole at the top of the gusset (at the point where the gusset meets the sock leg), pick up one or two extra stitches there.

Step 1: With the right side of the work facing you, insert a knitting needle into the first edge stitch of the heel flap. Bring the yarn round the needle as to knit, and draw the yarn through and up onto the needle. You have picked up one stitch.

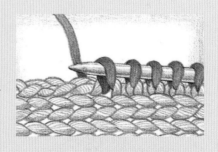

Step 2: Continue to pick up stitches in this manner across all remaining flap rows.

Ending the Sock

When working a top-down sock, you will end the work at the toe; when working from the toe up, you will end at the cuff or top of the sock. Different methods of ending the work are used depending on the type of sock.

KITCHENER STITCH

Kitchener stitch, or grafting, is used to close up the toe of a top-down sock. This method forms an invisible join and leaves no rough edges inside the sock.

Before grafting, you will have decreased to approximately 24 stitches and divided your stitches evenly onto two needles. Begin by cutting off the yarn, leaving a 12" tail. To prevent jagged corners at each end of the toe and to create a smooth, rounded toe, use this simple trick before grafting: decrease one stitch at each end of each needle by passing the first stitch on the needle over the second stitch.

To do this, slip the two right-hand stitches from the working needle to a spare needle. Pass the right-hand stitch over the left-hand stitch, and slip the remaining stitch back to the working needle. Turn the work, and do the same thing at the other end of the needle, working with the wrong side facing you. Repeat on both sides of the other working needle. You have decreased two stitches on each needle.

Now you're ready to graft. Thread the tail into a yarn needle. Hold the stitches as shown in the illustrations.

Step 1: Insert the yarn needle purlwise into the first stitch on the front needle and pull the yarn through, leaving the stitch on the knitting needle.

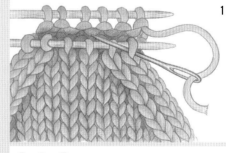

Step 2: Insert the tapestry needle knitwise through the first stitch on the back needle. Pull the yarn through, leaving the stitch on the knitting needle.

(continued on page 34)

Step 3: Insert the tapestry needle knitwise through the first stitch on the front needle, and slip the stitch off the needle. Insert the tapestry needle purlwise through the next stitch on the front needle, and pull the yarn through, leaving this stitch on the needle.

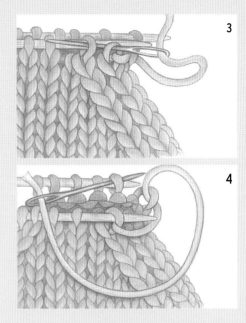

Step 4: Insert the tapestry needle purlwise through the first stitch on the back needle, and slip the stitch off the needle. Insert the tapestry needle knitwise through the next stitch on the back needle, and pull the yarn through, leaving this stitch on the knitting needle.

Repeat Steps 3 and 4 until all stitches on both knitting needles have been joined. Fasten off and weave in the yarn end.

BINDING OFF

If the sock is worked toe up, it will be necessary to bind off the last row of stitches. If you are working in ribbing, bind off in ribbing for a neat finish. Be sure to bind off loosely so that the top of the sock stretches to fit comfortably. Go up one or two needle sizes if necessary.

WEAVING IN YARN ENDS

When the sock is completed, turn it inside out and weave in the loose yarn ends. Using a yarn needle, weave the ends back and forth invisibly through the backs of stitches until they are secure. Never use knots!

Chapter 3
Anatomy of a Sock

The anatomy of a sock must, of course, follow the anatomy of the foot—that incredibly engineered structure that takes you from here to there and back hundreds of times a day. If you've ever had a blister or other foot problem, you know just how important it is to pamper your feet. Socks have been a necessity of life from the most ancient of days, providing protection, warmth and comfort.

But today with hand-knit socks, we go a step farther: we celebrate our feet by turning what could be mundane tubes into a fashion statement by adding color and texture. Today, socks are fun!

Socks can be knitted flat in rows, back and forth, then seamed; they can be knitted seamlessly in rounds on four or five double-pointed sock needles or on circular needles; they can be knitted starting at the top of the cuff and working down to the toe, or they can be started at the toe and knitted up to the cuff. They can be made with a rounded toe, a square toe or a swirled toe. They might have a square heel, a round heel or even no heel at all. But whatever way they are knitted, they all have the same basic structure.

The following paragraphs describe the techniques used to work a top-down sock. Later in the chapter, you'll find detailed instructions and illustrations for working both top-down and toe-up socks.

Parts of a Sock

Each sock has seven parts:

1. Cuff or Top Treatment

This is the part that holds the top to the leg so that the top does not slither down. It is often made in stretchy ribbing, plain or fancy, and the length can be varied. Elastic thread or round elastic can be worked with the yarn to ensure the stretch.

2. Leg

This is the part that covers the leg down to the start of the heel and is the area most visible when the sock is worn. This area is the main showcase for colorful or textured design elements.

3. Heel Flap

To create the heel flap, you work back and forth on approximately half the leg stitches (see page 38). The other half of the stitches rest while you work the heel flap and heel. The heel flap gets a lot of wear from shoes, so it is usually worked in a stitch pattern that adds some

durability, such as a slip-stitch pattern. Often additional fibers (such as Wooly Nylon) are added to make the flap more durable. Some sock yarns come with a tiny skein of reinforced thread that you use to knit the heel flap.

4. Turned Heel

Turning a heel simply means knitting a sort of "cup" in which the heel will fit. The process is called "turning" because most methods call for short rows that are turned frequently. Contrary to what you may have heard, turning a heel is actually an easy and fun process (see page 38).

5. Gusset

Once you turn the heel, you must rejoin the heel stitches to those resting stitches so that the foot can be completed. Pick up stitches along both edges of the heel flap, then join the heel stitches and the resting stitches and begin knitting in rounds once more.

Because of the picked-up stitches, you will now have more stitches on your needles than you had earlier. The gusset consists of a series of decrease rows in which you remove those extra stitches.

6. Foot

This is the part that covers the foot—the instep and the sole. Because this part is usually worn within a shoe, bumps and lumps in a pattern should be avoided.

The sock's foot should be worked to the exact length of the wearer's foot. Therefore, begin shaping the toe when the sock foot is about 2" shorter than the person's foot, measured from the back of the heel to the tip of the longest toe.

The sock's length is very important. If it is too long, the sock will bunch up in the shoe and create blisters. If it is too short, the toes will be cramped and painful.

7. Toe

There are many ways to shape a toe. The most common method is to work a series of paired decreases, each decrease row usually separated by an even row. The gradual narrowing of the piece creates a shaped toe. Most toe shapings are worked so that left and right socks are interchangeable.

And there you have it—a sock from top to toe!

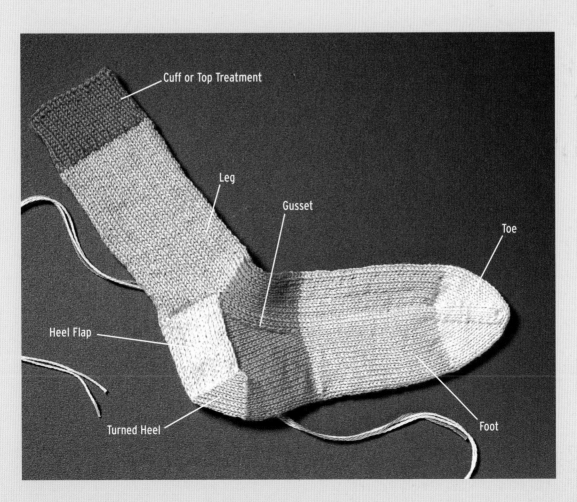

TURNING THE HEEL

Turning a sock heel has an unwarranted reputation for being difficult. Actually, it's easy and fun to create a heel. To help allay any fears, try working just a heel by itself to learn the technique. You'll need two straight needles and some yarn.

Sample Heel

Cast on 16 stitches.

Work the heel flap, a square piece that covers and protects the back of the heel and leads into the turning point.

Row 1 (RS): *Sl one as if to purl, k1; rep from * across. Turn.

Row 2: Purl across.

Rep Rows 1 and 2 six times more, then Row 1 one more time. The heel flap is now completed. Note how soft and cushy the slip-stitch pattern is.

Heel Turning

Ssk (slip, slip knit): Sl next 2 sts, one at a time, as to knit. Insert left needle through both sts from right to left, and K2tog: ssk made.

Row 1 (WS): p10, p2 tog, p1; turn, leaving last 3 sts unworked.

Row 2: Sl 1 knitwise, k5, ssk, k1; turn, leaving last 3 sts unworked.

Row 3: Sl 1 purlwise, p6, p2 tog, p1; turn, leaving last st unworked.

Row 4: Sl 1 knitwise, k7, ssk, k1; turn, leaving last st unworked.

Row 5: Sl 1 purlwise, p8, p2tog, turn.

Row 6: Sl 1 as to knit, k8, ssk.

And there it is—that dreaded turned heel! If this were a real sock, you would now go on to work the gussets on each side of the heel flap. But for this sample, you can now bind off and save the piece for reference.

Sock Construction

There are two basic ways to knit a sock in the round: from the top (cuff) down or from the toe up.

On the following pages, you will see the steps and techniques involved in each type of construction.

Construction of a Top-Down Sock

Step 1: The cuff of this sock has been knit in the round on five needles in a knit 1, purl 1 rib.

Step 2: The leg has been worked in plain stockinette stitch. The knitter is ready to divide for the heel.

Step 3: Half the stitches have been placed on one needle, and the heel flap has been worked back-and-forth in a slip-stitch pattern.

Step 4: About half the heel has been completed. Notice the paired decreases on both sides of the heel cup (see the basic heel pattern on page 38).

Step 5: The heel has been completed, and the knitter has picked up the stitches along one side of the heel flap. She will now rejoin the round, work across the two needles holding the foot stitches and pick up the stitches along the other side of the flap.

Step 6: The gusset has been completed, and the foot is being worked in rounds.

Step 7: To shape the toe, the knitter is working paired decreases on every other round.

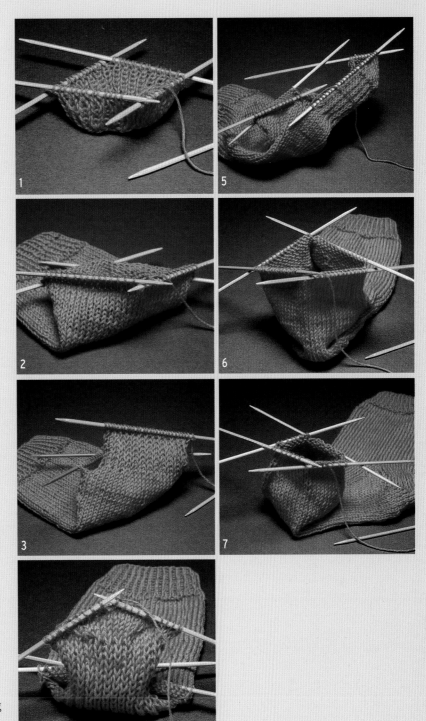

TOP-DOWN TOES AND HEELS

Top-down socks have many different toe and heel shapes, reflecting the great variety of sock traditions around the world and over time. The patterns in this book demonstrate many of these forms.

Heels

Several heel shapes are more widely used than others. For example, many designers use the "round heel," because of its strength and simplicity of working. The round heel is constructed by knitting a square heel flap and then working a series of short rows to "turn" the heel. The sample heel on page 38 is a classic round heel, and the Mosaic Socks (see page 92) have this kind of heel.

Mosaic Socks

There are many variations on the round heel. (An excellent reference work about toes and heels is Nancy Bush's book *Folk Socks*). For example, the half-handkerchief heel is similar to the round heel but has a narrower shape. Nancy Bush's Estonian Socks (see page 138) have a half-handkerchief heel.

Estonian Socks

The heel of a top-down sock can also be worked with short rows only, using a very small heel flap or with no heel flap at all. The garter-heel socks (see page 96) use this technique.

Garter Heel Socks

Toes

The most common toe shape for a top-down sock is a wedge toe. This is created by working paired decreases on both sides of the toe. The Leaf Lace Socks on page 107 use this type of toe.

Star toes and round toes are created by decreasing evenly around the toe rather than only on the two sides. Just like the top of a simple watch cap, both these toes are shaped by decreases spaced evenly all around the work. On a round toe, the decreases are close together and are worked every third, fourth or fifth row, so no prominent decrease lines appear. A star toe is similar, but it uses fewer decreases and more decrease rows, making the decrease lines quite prominent (see the Mosaic Socks). Both toes are finished off by gathering the remaining stitches together with a yarn needle

Leaf Lace Socks

Construction of a Toe-Up Sock

Step 1: The short-row toe has been worked. The knitter is in the process of picking up the wraps to return to the full number of live stitches. Note the provisional cast-on, worked in contrasting yarn.

Step 2: All stitches are evenly distributed on the four needles, and the knitter is halfway up the foot.

(continued on page 42)

Step 3: The short-row heel is worked in the same manner as the short-row toe.

Step 4: The knitter has completed the leg of the sock and is ready to bind off the cuff.

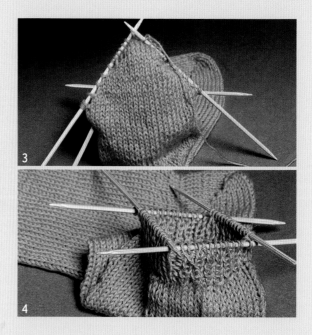

TOE-UP TOES AND HEELS

The toe and heel of a toe-up sock are identical to one another: both are constructed by beginning with half the total number of stitches, decreasing by working wrapped short rows and then picking up the wrapped stitches to increase to the full toe or heel width once again. See Chapter 2 for the short-row technique and the photos at right for the different stages of construction. Priscilla Gibson-Roberts gives the most complete explanation of the short-row technique in her book *Simple Socks: Plain and Fancy*, in which she uses the short-row toe and heel for both top-down and toe-up socks. Her Scandinavian Socks (see page 142) demonstrate graphically that short-row toes and heels are identical.

Scandinavian Socks

Chapter 4
Designing Socks

You've knitted a pair or two of socks from patterns, and you understand the basic construction of socks. Now you have an idea for a special pair you'd like to knit, but you just can't find the perfect pattern. What to do? Design your own, of course!

Designing socks is actually easy. You need to know how big the socks should be—the length and width. You need to choose a yarn and then calculate an accurate stitch gauge for it. You also need to know how socks are constructed and which method—top-down or toe-up—you prefer to use. Finally, you need a Sock Calculator—a formula you can use to write your pattern. In this chapter, we'll take you through all the steps of designing and writing your own sock pattern. We've provided two Universal Sock Patterns, one for top-down socks and one for toe-up socks.

Taking Measurements

Begin by making a photocopy of the Sock Worksheet on page 175. Use it to note measurements and other key information along the way.

Let's assume your first designing adventure is for a pair of toe-up socks worked in the round on five needles in stockinette stitch. For most ankle-length socks, you'll need to use a tape measure to measure around the foot at its widest point. This width will determine how many stitches are required. Check the width around the largest part of the ankle as well—you'll probably find that it's the same as the foot width, or only slightly different. If it's very different, however, you'll need to adjust the number of stitches you cast on to compensate.

The length of the foot is the second critical measurement. Stand on a piece of blank paper while barefoot, and place a mark at the back of the heel and at the tip of the longest toe. Draw a straight line between these two points, and you have the foot length of your sock. Note these measurements on the Sock Worksheet.

Choosing Yarn

Traditionally, wool has been the fiber of choice for knitting socks. It is warm and has great shape memory, or elasticity, meaning that wool socks fit well. Wool is still a favorite, but today's knitter has a wide choice of natural fibers, including silk, cotton, bamboo, soy, alpaca, mohair and cashmere, as well as yarns containing nylon or acrylic.

In choosing sock yarn, consider durability. Some of the more fragile yarns can be supplemented by using a carry-along reinforcing yarn, such as Wooly Nylon, at the major wear points such as heels and toes. Some sock yarns, especially those produced in Europe, come with a spool of reinforcing thread to knit into these key wear points.

Sock yarns are relatively fine: usually fingering, baby or sportweight. They are usually characterized as 1 (super-fine) or 2 (fine) according to the Craft Yarn Council's standard yarn weight system (see craftyarncouncil.com). You can use thicker yarns, but socks made from them may not be comfortable when worn with shoes.

Gauges of 7 to 8 stitches per inch are common, worked on size 0 to 3 (2mm to 3.25mm) knitting needles. Socks that are too small or too large will be uncomfortable when worn, so maintaining gauge is important.

Elasticity is also important, especially in sock ribbing. Yarns like cotton or alpaca, which don't have a great deal of natural stretch memory, can be worked with a carry-along strand of fine elastic for the ribbing.

For warmth, pure wool is a good choice as it can absorb a great deal of moisture and still feel warm. Superwash wools make caring for socks easy. A yarn that is spun of

This sock is knitted from Louet Sales Gems Sportweight, a 100 percent wool yarn.

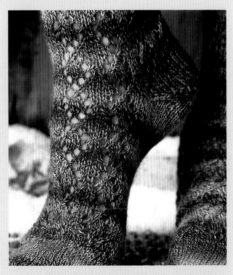

This sock is knitted from Zitron/Skacel Collection Inc. Trekking XXL, a sock yarn made of 75 percent wool and 25 percent nylon.

SOCK YARN CHART (by weight)

SUPERFINE yarn weight: (1)

Company	Yarn	Fiber Content	Gauge/4"	Needle Size
Austermann	Step	75% wool, 25% nylon	30 st	1, 2
Blue Moon Fiber Arts	Socks That Rock	100% superwash merino	32 sts	1
Brown Sheep Company	Wildfoote Luxury Sock Yarn	75% washable wool, 25% nylon	32 sts	1
Claudia Hand Painted Yarns	Fingering Weight	100% merino wool	26-30 sts	2, 3
Crystal Palace Yarns	Panda Cotton	55% bamboo, 24% cotton, 21% elastic nylon	28-32 sts	2
Dale of Norway	Baby Ull	100% superwash merino	32 sts	1, 2
Fleece Artist	Merino	100% superwash merino	28 sts	1
Interlacements	Tiny Toes	100% superwash merino	28 sts	2
Koigu Wool Designs	KPPPM	100% merino wool	28 sts	3
Koigu Wool Designs	KPM	100% merino wool	28 sts	3
Lang	Jawoll Cotton	49% new wool, 35% cotton, 16% nylon	28 sts	3
Lang	Jawoll	75% new wool, 18% nylon, 7% acrylic	30 sts	2, 3
Lorna's Laces	Shepherd Sock	75% wool, 25% nylon	28 sts	1
Louet Sales	Gems Fingering Weight	100% merino wool	26-30 sts	2, 3
Lana Grossa/Unicorn Books & Crafts	Mielenweit	80% wool, 20% nylon	28 sts	2, 3
OnLine/KFI	Supersocke Highland Color	75% superwash wool, 25% polyamide	30 sts	2
OnLine/KFI	Supersocke Sierra Color	75% superwash wool, 25% polyamide	30 sts	2
OnLine/KFI	Supersocke Walking Color	75% superwash wool, 25% polyamide	30 sts	2
Opal	Opal 4ply	75% superwash wool, 25% polyamide	32 sts	1
Ornaghi Filati	Luna Park	100% superwash wool	32 sts	2, 3
Plymouth Yarn Co.	Sockotta Sock Yarn	45% cotton, 40% superwash wool, 15% nylon	28 sts	2
Regia/Schachenmayr Nomotta/Westminster Fibers, Inc.	Tip Top Color	41% new wool, 34% cotton, 25% polyamid	30 sts	3
Regia/Schachenmayr Nomotta/Westminster Fibers, Inc.	4Fädig	75% wool, 25% polyamide	30 sts	1, 2
Regia/Schachenmayr Nomotta/Westminster Fibers, Inc.	Bamboo	45% bamboo, 40% wool, 15% nylon	30 sts	3

SUPERFINE

SUPERFINE yarn weight: 1

Company	Yarn	Fiber Content	Gauge/4"	Needle Size
Rowan/Westminster Fibers, Inc.	4ply Soft	100% merino wool	28 sts	3
Rowan/Westminster Fibers, Inc.	Scottish Tweed 4ply	100% merino wool	26-28 sts	2, 3
Schoeller & Stahl/Skacel Collection, Inc.		75% superwash wool, 25% nylon	30 sts	2,3
Schoolhouse Press	Satakieli	100% wool	24-32 sts	1
Schaefer Yarn Company	Anne	60% merino wool superwash, 25% mohair, 15% nylon	28 sts	1
Shelridge Farms	Soft Touch Ultra	100% superwash wool	28 sts	3
The Great Adirondack Yarn Co.	Soxie	100 merino wool superwash	28 sts	2
The Great Adirondack Yarn Co.	Silky Sock	70% merino wool, 20% silk, 10% nylon	32sts	3
Zitron/Skacel Collection, Inc.	Trekking XXL	75% wool, 25% nylon	28 sts	2, 3

FINE yarn weight: 2

Company	Yarn	Fiber Content	Gauge/4"	Needle Size
Artyarns	Ultramerino 4	100% merino wool	27 sts	4
Brown Sheep Co.	Cotton Fine	80% cotton, 20% wool	26 sts	2
Cherry Tree Hill Yarn	Supersock	100% superwash merino	26 sts	3
Crystal Palace Yarns	Kid Merino	28% kid mohair, 28% merino wool, 44% micro nylon	various	3, 4, 5
Lion Brand Yarn	Magic Stripes	75% wool, 25% nylon	24 sts	4
Lorna's Laces	Shepherd Sport	100% superwash merino	24 sts	4
Louet Sales	Gems Sport Weight	100% merino wool	20-24 sts	3, 4, 5
Mountain Colors	Bearfoot	60% superwash wool, 25% mohair, 15% nylon	20-24 sts	3, 4
Opal	Opal 6ply	75% superwash wool, 25% polyamide	24 sts	3, 4, 5

LIGHT yarn weight: 3

Company	Yarn	Fiber Content	Gauge/4"	Needle Size
Cascade Yarns	Fixation	98.3% cotton, 1.7% elastic	22 sts	5, 6, 7, 8, 9
Interlacements	Toasty Toes	100% superwash merino	24 sts	6
Louet Sales	Gems Worsted Weight	100% merino wool	18-20 sts	5, 6, 7
Mountain Colors	Twizzle	85% merino wool, 15% silk	16-20 sts	4, 5, 6

100 percent synthetic fiber does not absorb moisture and will not keep your feet warm.

Sock yarns are easily substituted, as long as the new yarn can be worked to the exact gauge as the original. But note that in substituting there may be differences in elasticity, texture or moisture absorption. See the Sock Yarn Chart on pages 46–47.

The color palette available in sock yarns is practically unlimited. Many sock knitters say their choice of yarn is often determined by color over any other feature.

How Much Yarn?

You will need approximately 350 yards/315 meters of superfine sock yarn to make a pair of socks for an adult—slightly less for a woman, slightly more for most men. Conveniently, most sock yarns are sold in skeins of around 175 or 350 yards/158 or 315 meters. You will learn from experience how much yarn to buy, and when you are starting out, your yarn shop owner will be able to offer advice. If your pattern includes colorwork or cables, you may need as much as 50 percent more yarn than you would use to knit a plain pair of socks.

Self-Striping Yarns

When the first self-striping and self-patterning yarns hit the market, sock knitters found an exciting new world at their fingertips! These yarns are dyed or painted so that when knitted, they automatically form stripes or other patterns.

Sock knitters were delighted to find themselves suddenly creating stripes, checks and other designs

This sock is knitted from Schoeller & Stahl/Skacel Collection, Inc. Fortissima Colori, a self-patterning sock yarn. The stripes and "Fair Isle" patterns are dyed into the yarn.

without having to change colors. The actual patterns formed may vary depending on needle size, gauge or number of stitches being worked.

In order to make a pair of identical socks, begin each sock at the exact same point of the yarn's color sequence. Otherwise, you may end up with fraternal rather than identical twin socks, which can be quite fun and interesting if planned but unpleasantly surprising if not.

The self-striping yarns come in wonderful color combinations, from bright and vibrant to softly muted. These yarns can be combined with appropriate solids for working gussets and heels or even for ribbing and toes.

The self-striping yarns look their best when worked in stockinette stitch or other simple stitches. When used in cable or other textured patterns, the look of the pattern stitches can be completely lost. They also do not work well with ornate lace patterns matched with a solid.

It's fun to use a self-striping yarn and watch the patterns develop as you knit. Give them a try, and see if they speak to you.

Caring for Hand-Knitted Socks

For your precious hand-knitted socks, as for all other hand-knits, the most important step in care is to read the care instructions on the yarn label.

Superwash wools and some synthetic fibers can be laundered in a washing machine, but even these may look and wear better if air-dried.

Wool and other natural fibers need to be hand washed in a mild soap (never detergent), rolled in a towel to remove excess moisture, then patted into shape on a dry towel until drying is completed. Most socks don't need to be blocked, but commercial blocking forms in the shape of the foot and leg are available. Sometimes vintage sock blocking forms can be found in antique shops. You can also cut out a sock form from foam board, then cover it in plastic wrap or aluminum foil. This is economical if you knit socks in several sizes.

Calculating Gauge

Gauge is critical for sock knitting. Using the correct gauge can be the difference between a well-fitting pair of socks and a shapeless mess. **Always knit a gauge swatch in the pattern you plan to use for your socks, using the yarn and needles you've selected**. Socks should be knitted rather densely for durability and elasticity. A general rule when making socks is to use a smaller needle size than the one recommended for the yarn.

Some knitters feel that the gauge swatch for a garment to be knitted in the round should be knitted in the round as well; others feel that knitting a flat swatch is sufficient. It's most important to knit a swatch in the round if your stitch pattern is a complicated one. In this case, your gauge swatch may have as many stitches as you intend to use for the sock itself. If you feel a flat swatch will do, make it at least 4 inches/10 centimeters square, bind off and measure the gauge as illustrated.

Measuring Gauge

Note the gauge on the Sock Worksheet. No matter how you measured your gauge before beginning your socks, always check gauge again once you've completed half of the leg (for a top-down sock) or half of the foot (for a toe-up sock).

How Many Stitches?

Once you've determined your gauge and the width of your sock, you can figure out how many stitches you'll need to fit around the foot and leg. Use this gauge formula:

$$\frac{Stitches}{per\ inch} \quad X \quad \frac{Foot}{circumference} \quad = \quad \frac{Number}{of\ stitches}$$

For example, if your gauge is 8 stitches per inch and your foot is 8 inches around, you would have approximately 64 stitches around the leg and foot. For a top-down sock, you would cast on this number of stitches. For a toe-up sock, you would cast on approximately half this number, or 32 stitches. Choose the pattern size that's closest to the number of stitches you need.

One final consideration affects how many stitches you cast on: how do you want the sock to fit? If you're knitting with an elastic fiber such as wool, in a stretchy pattern such as ribbing, and you want the sock to fit snugly, you may want to cast on as few as 75 percent of the number of stitches the gauge requires. In the example above, that would be around 48 stitches instead of 64. If, however, you are knitting in a stranded color pattern such as a Fair Isle, or a fairly nonelastic pattern and yarn, such as a stockinette-stitch sock made of cotton yarn, you might start with the full number of stitches as determined by the gauge formula.

Vogue®Knitting Sock Calculator and Universal Patterns

On the opposite page you will find the Vogue Knitting Sock Calculator, a table that you can use to create a pattern for socks of any size from baby through adult extra-large, using yarn of any gauge from superfine weight through DK weight and worked in the stitch pattern of your choice (see chapter 5). To design your own custom socks, use the Sock Calculator together with either of the two patterns that follow on the next pages: the Vogue Knitting Universal Toe-Up Sock Pattern and the Vogue Knitting Universal Top-Down Sock Pattern.

To use the Sock Calculator and either Universal Sock Pattern, substitute the number of stitches given in the calculator for the letters in the pattern. For example, suppose you are knitting a toe-up sock, in superfine yarn, in an adult size medium. The first line of the Universal Toe-Up Sock Pattern reads, "Using provisional crochet cast on, cast on C sts." In the Sock Calculator table, in Column C, under superfine weight, size medium, you find the number 30. So you would cast on 30 stitches.

Using these tools, you can design socks that are as plain or as fancy as you like. Make stockinette-stitch socks using a beautiful variegated yarn,

VOGUE®KNITTING SOCK CALCULATOR

SUPERFINE YARN—7½ to 8 stitches and 11 to 12½ rows per inch on size 0-1 (2-2.25mm) needles

	A	B	C	D	E	F	G	H	I
Size	CO sts	Ribbing	Heel sts	Leg length	Rows for heel flap	Rem heel sts	Pick-up gusset sts	Foot length to toe shaping	Rem toe sts
Baby	40	1"/2.5cm	20	2¾"/7cm	21	12	11	4½"/11.5cm	16
Child 1-2	44	1"/2.5cm	22	3"/7.5cm	23	14	12	5"/12.5cm	16
Child 3-4	44	1"/2.5cm	22	3¼"/8.5cm	23	14	12	5½"/14cm	16
Child 6-8	48	1½"/4cm	24	4½"/11.5cm	25	14	13	5¾"/14.5cm	20
Child 10-12	56	1½"/4cm	28	5¼"/13.5cm	29	16	15	6"/15cm	20
Adult XS	60	1½"/4cm	30	6"/15cm	31	18	16	6¼"/16cm	20
Adult S	60	1½"/4cm	30	6"/15cm	31	18	16	7"/18cm	20
Adult M	60	1½"/4cm	30	6"/15cm	31	18	16	7¼-8"/18.5-20.5cm	20
Adult L	64	2"/5cm	32	8"/20cm	33	18	17	8¼-9"/21-23cm	24
Adult XL	72	2"/5cm	36	8"/20cm	37	20	19	9¼-10"/23.5-24.5cm	28

FINE YARN—6½ to 7 stitches and 8½ to 9 rows per inch on size 2-3 (2.75-3.25mm)needles

	A	B	C	D	E	F	G	H	I
Size	CO sts	Ribbing	Heel sts	Leg length	Rows for heel flap	Rem heel sts	Pick-up gusset sts	Foot length to toe shaping	Rem toe sts
Baby	32	1"/2.5cm	16	2¾"/7cm	17	10	9	4½"/11.5cm	12
Child 1-2	32	1"/2.5cm	16	3"/7.5cm	17	10	9	5"/12.5cm	12
Child 3-4	32	1"/2.5cm	16	3¼"/8.5cm	17	10	9	5½"/14cm	16
Child 6-8	36	1½"/4cm	18	4½"/11.5cm	19	12	10	5¾"/14.5cm	16
Child 10-12	44	1½"/4cm	22	5¼"/13.5cm	23	14	12	6"/15cm	16
Adult XS	48	1½"/4cm	24	6"/15cm	25	14	13	6¼"/16cm	16
Adult S	48	1½"/4cm	24	6"/15cm	25	14	13	7"/18cm	20
Adult M	48	1½"/4cm	24	6"/15cm	25	14	13	7¼-8"/18.5-20.5cm	20
Adult L	52	2"/5cm	26	8"/20cm	27	16	14	8¼-9"/21-23cm	20
Adult XL	56	2"/5cm	28	8"/20cm	29	16	15	9¼-10"/23.5-24.5cm	20

DK-WEIGHT YARN—5½ to 6 stitches and 7 to 8 rows per inch on size 4-5 (3.5-3.75mm) needles

	A	B	C	D	E	F	G	H	I
Size	CO sts	Ribbing	Heel sts	Leg length	Rows for heel flap	Rem heel sts	Pick-up gusset sts	Foot length to toe shaping	Rem toe sts
Baby	28	1"/2.5cm	14	2¾"/7cm	15	10	8	4½"/11.5cm	12
Child 1-2	32	1"/2.5cm	16	3"/7.5cm	17	10	9	5"/12.5cm	12
Child 3-4	32	1"/2.5cm	16	3¼"/8.5cm	17	10	9	5½"/14cm	16
Child 6-8	32	1½"/4cm	16	4½"/11.5cm	17	10	9	5¾"/14.5cm	16
Child 10-12	36	1½"/4cm	18	5¼"/13.5cm	19	12	10	6"/15cm	16
Adult XS	40	1½"/4cm	20	6"/15cm	21	12	11	6¼"/16cm	16
Adult S	40	1½"/4cm	20	6"/15cm	21	12	11	7"/18cm	20
Adult M	40	1½"/4cm	20	6"/15cm	21	12	11	7¼-8"/18.5-20.5cm	20
Adult L	44	2"/5cm	22	8"/20cm	23	14	12	8¼-9"/21-23cm	20
Adult XL	48	2"/5cm	24	8"/20cm	25	14	13	9¼-10"/23.5-24.5cm	20

socks with a simple rib pattern or socks with a lace or colorwork pattern (but be sure to determine your gauge in your chosen stitch pattern). Vary the leg length and top treatment in any way you wish.

In Chapter 5, you'll find over 50 stitch patterns, complete with charts and directions, all written specifically for knitting in the round. To design socks with a fancy stitch pattern, select one that has a number of stitches that divides evenly into the total number of stitches for the leg of your sock. For example, if the leg of your sock will have 60 stitches, choose a stitch pattern with a repeat of 2, 3, 5, 6, 10, 12 or 15 stitches.

Finally, use the Sock Worksheet at the back of this book to note the desired measurements of your sock, the knitting method (top-down or toe-up), the yarn and gauge, the stitch pattern and other key information. Using all these tools, you will be able to create unique socks of any type you choose.

Vogue® Knitting Universal Toe-Up Sock Pattern

This pattern creates a classic toe-up sock with a short-row heel and toe. See Chapters 2 and 3 for techniques.

TOE
Using provisional crochet cast-on (see Chapter 2), cast on C sts.
Row 1 (WS) Purl to end, turn.
*Row 2 K to last 2 sts, WT.
Row 3 P to last 2 sts, WT.
Row 4 K to 1 st before last wrapped st, WT.
Row 5 P to 1 st before last wrapped st, WT.
Rep rows 4 and 5 until there are [half of I] unwrapped sts.

Row 1 K to next wrapped st, WW, WT.
Row 2 P to next wrapped st, WW, WT.
Rep rows 1 and 2 until both end sts have been wrapped.
Next row K to wrapped st, WW.**

FOOT
Carefully remove waste yarn and place C sts evenly divided onto 2 needles (pick up an extra stitch if necessary) and k across—A sts. Place marker for end of rnd. Work even in St st on next C sole sts (working WW on first st only), and in pat st on foll C instep sts until foot measures I from toe.

HEEL
Work same as toe, from * to **, over C sts of sole.

LEG
Work in pat st to wrapped st (beg of rnd). WW, cont in pat st for D.

CUFF
Work in rib for B. Bind off loosely in rib.

Vogue Knitting Universal Top-Down Sock Pattern

This pattern creates a classic sock with a round heel and a wedge toe. See Chapter 3 for information about different heel and toe shapes.

CUFF

Cast on A sts and divide evenly onto 4 needles. Join, being careful not to twist sts. Place marker for end of rnd (between needles 4 and 1) and sl marker every rnd. Work in desired rib for B.

LEG

Work in pat st for D.

HEEL

Heel is worked over half the total number of sts— Needles 1 and 4 combined onto one needle.

Heel flap

With Needle 4, work sts on Needle 1 (C sts on one needle). Turn.

Row 1 Purl C, turn.

Row 2 (RS) *Sl 1, k1; rep from * to end, turn.

Row 3 Sl 1, p to end, turn.

Rep rows 2 and 3 until there are a total of E rows.

Turn heel

Mark center of heel.

Row 1 (RS) Sl 1, k to 2 sts past center, ssk, k1, turn.

Row 2 Sl 1, p5, p2tog, p1, turn.

Row 3 Sl 1, k to 1 st before gap, ssk (closing gap), k1, turn.

Row 4 Sl 1, p to 1 st before gap, p2tog (closing gap), p1, turn.

Rep rows 3 and 4 until all sts have been worked, omitting k1 and p1 at end of last 2 rows when necessary—F sts.

GUSSETS

With a spare dpn, k half of F. With Needle 1, k half of F, pick up and k G sts along side of heel flap; with Needles 2 and 3, cont in pattern across C instep sts; with Needle 4, pick up and k G sts along side of heel flap, k half of F—total number of sts = F + G + G + C. Place marker for end of rnd.

Shape gussets

Rnd 1 For Needle 1, k to last 3 sts, k2tog, k1; for Needles 2 and 3, cont in pattern; for Needle 4, k1, ssk, k to end.

Rnd 2 Work even in St st on Needles 1 and 4; work even in pattern on Needles 2 and 3.

Rep rnds 1 and 2 until there are A sts.

FOOT

Cont even in Pats as established until foot measures H from back of heel.

TOE

Rnd 1 *For Needle 1, k to last 3 sts, k2tog, k1; for Needle 2, k1, ssk, k to end; rep from * for Needles 3 and 4.

Rnd 2 Knit.

Rep rnds 1 and 2 until there are I sts.

FINISHING

With Needle 4, k sts from Needle 1. Slip sts from Needle 2 onto Needle 3.

Graft toe sts using Kitchener st (see Chapter 2).

Weave in ends.

Chapter 5
Stitch Patterns for Socks

This chapter includes nearly 60 stitch patterns of

all types—ribs, lace, cables and colorwork—that

are appropriate for sock designs. This is just a

sample of the many thousands of stitch patterns

available; you can consult pattern dictionaries,

such as the Stitchionary series (Sixth&Spring

Books), Barbara Walker's series of Treasuries

(Schoolhouse Press) or the Harmony Guides,

for many more.

When selecting a stitch pattern for a pair of socks, keep a few factors in mind:

• **Scale** Because socks are small, choose a pattern with a relatively narrow repeat rather than a wide cable or lace panel. All the patterns in this chapter have repeats of 15 stitches or less.

• **Yarn** Choose a pattern that will work well with the yarn you intend to use. For example, cables and ribs are springier and have more elasticity when worked in wool rather than in cotton; highly variegated yarns are best used with simple stitch patterns.

• **Gauge** You will get a different gauge in most stitch patterns than in stockinette, even using the same yarn and needles. To make sure your socks fit properly, work your gauge swatch in the stitch pattern you plan to use (see Chapter 4 for more information on gauge).

• **Stitch Multiple** When adding a stitch pattern to your basic sock, find one with a multiple that will fit within the stitch count of the sock. For example, a 64-stitch sock will accept stitch patterns with multiples of 2, 4, 8, 16 or 32 stitches. If there's a pattern you like that doesn't quite fit, a few stitches added to or subtracted from the basic sock pattern will not affect the fit too much.

The patterns and charts in this chapter are adapted for circular knitting, so they all work well for the leg portion of a sock. The foot is a different story, however: because many sock knitters like to knit in pattern across the instep but keep the sole of the foot plain, you will need to make some small adjustments in most patterns before knitting the foot of your sock. In most cases, you will add a stitch or two so that the pattern is balanced on both sides. For example, in the Garter Ridge Rib (next page), you would add one purl stitch at the beginning of the pattern round to balance the purl

stitch at the end; in the Tiny Eyelet Rib (page 58), you would add three balancing stitches at the end of the last pattern repeat; for Chunky Cable Rib (page 71), add one purl stitch at the beginning; for Peas and Carrots (page 63), add another two-stitch repeat of the orange checks at the end.

Similar small adjustments are necessary in the number of stitches to be worked for the heel portions of many socks. For example, suppose you are working a top-down sock using the Chunky Cable Rib pattern (see page 71), and the leg has 70 stitches, or 10 complete pattern repeats. When you divide for the heel, you will need to set aside 36 instep stitches (5 full repeats plus one stitch to balance the pattern) and work the heel flap on 34 stitches instead of 35 (half the total number of stitches).

For another example, suppose you are working that same sock using the Tiny Eyelet Rib pattern (see page 58), and you have 65 stitches, or 13 pattern repeats, on the needles. When you divide for the heel, you must decide whether you want 6 or 7 pattern repeats (30 or 35 stitches) on the instep. If you choose 6 pattern repeats, you would add 3 balancing stitches to the instep stitches, giving you a total of 33 stitches on the instep. That leaves 32 stitches for the heel.

Sometimes making adjustments results in an odd number of stitch for the heel flap. In this case, increase or decrease one stitch to retain an even number of stiches. Such a small adjustment in the number of stitches will not affect the fit of the sock.

Ribbings

PURL RIDGES

(Multiple of 2 sts)

Rnds 1 and 2 Knit.

Rnd 3 *K1, p1; rep from * to end.

Rnd 4 Knit.

Rep rnds 1–4.

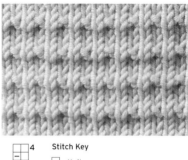

		4
−		
		1

2-st rep

Stitch Key

☐ Knit

⊟ Purl

GARTER RIDGE RIB

(Multiple of 3 sts)

Rnds 1, 2 and 3 *K2, p1; rep from * to end.

Rnd 4 Purl.

Rep rnds 1–4.

−	−	−	4
			1

4-st rep

Stitch Key

☐ Knit

⊟ Purl

BIG BAMBOO

(Multiple of 12 sts)

Rnds 1, 2, 3 and 4 *K4, p2; rep from * to end.

Rnds 5 and 6 *K4, p8; rep from * to end.

Rnds 7, 8, 9 and 10 Rep rnd 1.

Rnds 11 and 12 *P6, k4, p2; rep from * to end.

Rep rnds 1–12.

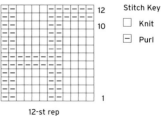

12-st rep

Stitch Key

☐ Knit

⊟ Purl

CARTRIDGE RIB

(Multiple of 5 sts)

Rnd 1 *K3, p1, k1; rep from * to end.

Rnd 2 *K2, p3; rep from * to end.

Rep rnds 1 and 2.

5-st rep

Stitch Key

☐ Knit

⊟ Purl

BRIOCHE RIB

(Multiple of 2 sts)

Rnd 1 Purl.

Rnd 2 *K1, k1 in row below; rep from * to end.

Rnd 3 *P1 in row below, p1; rep from * to end.

Rep rnds 2 and 3, end with rnd 2.

2-row rep
Prep rnd

2-st rep

Stitch Key

☐ Knit

⊟ Purl

Ⓝ K1 in row below

Ⓐ P1 in row below

TWISTED STITCH RIB

(Multiple of 3 sts)

LT With RH needle behind work, k 2nd st on LH needle tbl, leave st on needle, then k first st through front lp, sl both sts from needle.

RT With RH needle in front of work, k 2nd st on LH needle, leave st on needle, then k first st tbl, sl both sts from needle.

Rnd 1 *LT, p1; rep from * to end.

Rnd 2 *RT, p1; rep from * to end.

Rep rnds 1 and 2.

3-st rep

Stitch Key

⊠ LT

⊠ RT

⊟ Purl

LACE RIB

(Multiple of 6 sts)

Rnds 1 and 3 *P1, k2; rep from * to end.

Rnd 2 *P1, yo, ssk, p1, k2; rep from * to end.

Rnd 4 *P1, k2tog, yo, p1, k2; rep from * to end.

Rep rnds 1–4.

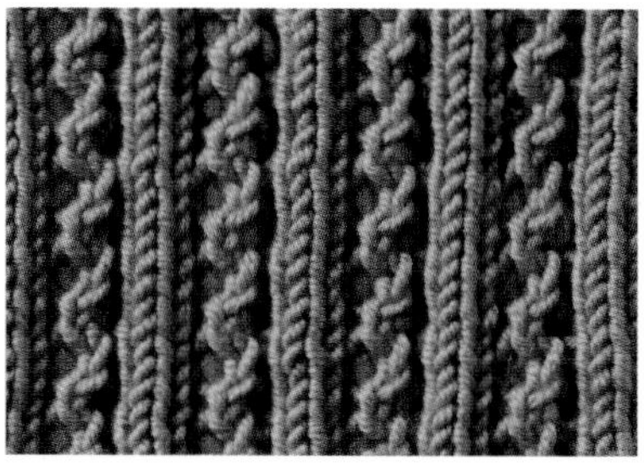

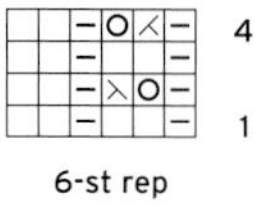
4
1
6-st rep

Stitch Key

- Knit
- Purl
- Yo
- Ssk
- K2tog

TINY EYELET RIB

(Multiple of 5 sts)

Prep rnd *P1, k1 tbl, p1, k2; rep from * to end.

Rnd 1 *P1, k1 tbl, p1, k2; rep from * to end.

Rnd 2 *P1, k1 tbl, p1, k1, yo, k1; rep from * to end.

Rnd 3 *P1, k1 tbl, p1, k3; rep from * to end.

Rnd 4 *P1, k1 tbl, p1, k3, pass the 3rd st on RH needle over the center 2 sts; rep from * to end.

Rep rnds 1–4.

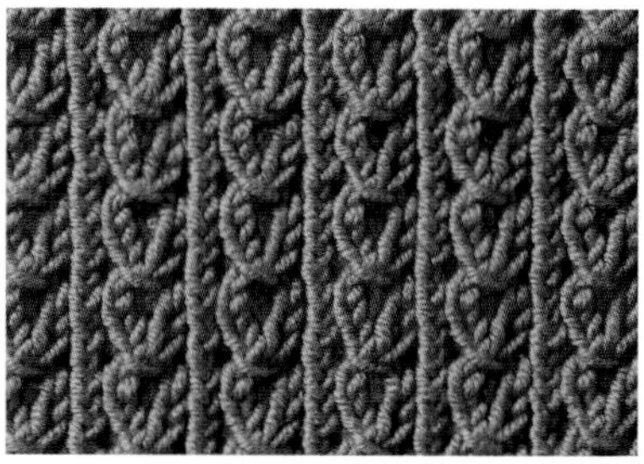

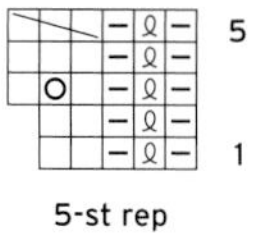
5
1
5-st rep

Stitch Key

- Knit
- K1 tbl
- Purl
- Yo
- K3, pass 3rd st on RH needle over center 2 sts

SLIP-STITCH WAFFLE RIB

(Multiple of 4 sts)

Rnd 1 *Sl 1, k3; rep from * to end.

Rnds 2, 4, 6 and 8 *K1, p3; rep from * to end.

Rnds 3, 5 and 7 *Wyib sl 1, p3; rep from * to end.

Rnd 9 Rep rnd 1.

Rnd 10 Purl.

Rep rnds 1–10.

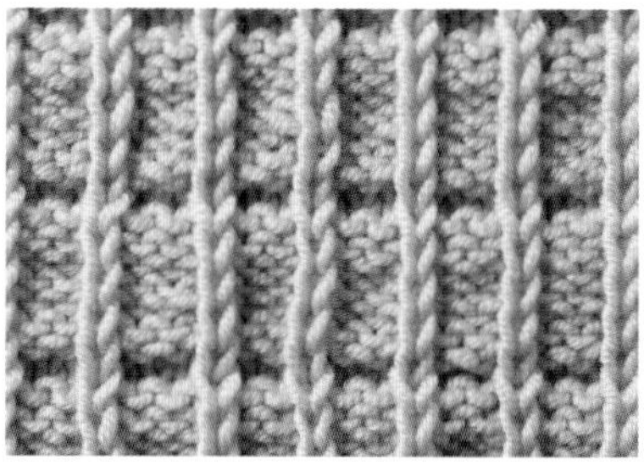

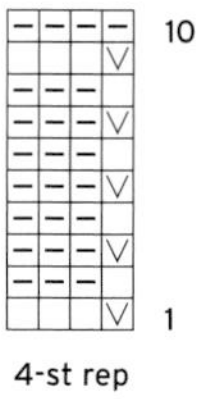
10
1
4-st rep

Stitch Key

- Knit
- Purl
- Wyib sl 1

VINE RIB

(Multiple of 15 sts)

RPT Sl 1 st to cn and hold to back, k1, p1 from cn.

LPT Sl 1 to cn and hold to front, p1, k1 from cn.

Rnds 1 and 2 *K4 tbl, p4, k3 tbl, p4; rep from * to end.

Rnd 3 *K4 tbl, p3, RPT, k1 tbl, LPT, p3; rep from * to end.

Rnd 4 *K4 tbl, p3, [k1 tbl, p1] 3 times, p2; rep from * to end.

Rnd 5 *K4 tbl, p2, RPT, p1, k1 tbl, p1, LPT, p2; rep from * to end.

Rnd 6 *K4 tbl, p2, [k1 tbl, p2] 3 times; rep from * to end.

Rnd 7 *K4 tbl, p1, RPT, p2, k1 tbl, p2, LPT, p1; rep from * to end.

Rnd 8 *K4 tbl, p1, [k1 tbl, p3] twice, k1 tbl, p1; rep from * to end.

Rnd 9 *K4 tbl, RPT, p3, k1 tbl, p3, LPT; rep from * to end.

Rnd 10 *K5 tbl, [p4, k1 tbl] twice; rep from * to end.

Rep rnds 1–10.

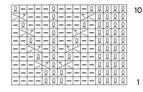

15-st rep

Stitch Key

Q	K1 tbl
—	Purl
⧅	RPT
⧄	LPT

GINGERBREAD RIB

(Multiple of 10 sts)

4-st LC Sl 2 sts to cn and hold to front, k2, k2 from cn.

Rnds 1 and 5 *P1, k4; rep from * to end.

Rnds 2 and 4 *P1, k4, p1, k1, p2, k1; rep from * to end.

Rnd 3 *P1, 4-st LC, p1, k4; rep from * to end.

Rnd 6 Rep rnd 2.

Rep rnds 1–6.

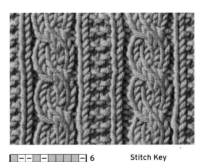

10-st rep

Stitch Key

☐	K
—	P
⧓	4-st LC

Texture Stitches

PIE CRUST BASKETWEAVE

(Multiple of 8 sts)

Rnds 1, 2 and 3 *P6, k2; rep from * to end.

Rnd 4 Knit.

Rnds 5, 6 and 7 *P2, k2, p4; rep from * to end.

Rnd 8 Knit.

Rep rnds 1–8.

8

1

8-st rep

Stitch Key

☐ Knit

⊟ Purl

SMALL MOCK BROCADE PLEATS

(Multiple of 7 sts)

Rnd 1 *P6, k1; rep from * to end.

Rnd 2 *P5, k2; rep from * to end.

Rnd 3 *P4, k3; rep from * to end.

Rnd 4 *P3, k4; rep from * to end.

Rnd 5 *P2, k5; rep from * to end.

Rnd 6 *P1, k6; rep from * to end.

Rep rnds 1–6.

6

1

7-st rep

Stitch Key

☐ Knit

⊟ Purl

OAT STITCH

(Multiple of 4 sts)

Pfb Purl in back and front of next st

Rnds 1, 3 and 5 *K2, [pfb] twice; rep from * to end.

Rnds 2, 4 and 6 *K2, [p2tog] twice; rep from * to end.

Rnds 7, 9 and 11 *[Pfb] twice, k2; rep from * to end.

Rnds 8, 10 and 12 *[P2tog] twice, k2; rep from * to end.

Rep rnds 1–12.

Stitch Key

☐ Knit

◢ P2tog

Ƹ Pfb

4-st rep

BLACKBERRY STITCH

(Multiple of 4 sts)

Rnds 1 and 3 Purl.

Rnd 2 *P3tog, [p1, k1, p1] in next st; rep from * to end.

Rnd 4 *[P1, k1, p1] in next st, p3tog; rep from * to end.

Rep rnds 1–4.

4-st rep

Stitch Key

Ψ [P1, k1, p1] in same st

☐ Purl

◢ P3tog

■ No Stitch

STRIPEY

Colors A and B

(Worked over any number of sts)

Rnd 1 With B, knit.

Rnds 2, 3 and 4 With B, purl.

Rnds 5-10 With A, knit.

Rep rnds 1–10.

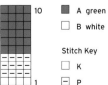

■ A green

☐ B white

Stitch Key

☐ K

☐ P

worked over any number of sts

SHADOW BOXING

Colors A and B

(Multiple of 2 sts)

Rnds 1 and 2 With A, purl.

Rnd 3 With B, *k1, wyib sl 1; rep from * to end.

Rnd 4 With B, *p1, wyib sl 1; rep from * to end.

Rnd 5 With A, *yo, k2tog; rep from * to end.

Rnd 6 With A, knit.

Rep rnds 1–6.

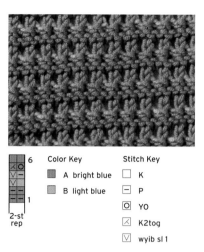

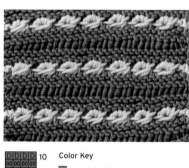

Color Key
- ■ A bright blue
- ■ B light blue

Stitch Key
- □ K
- ⊟ P
- Ⓞ YO
- ⊠ K2tog
- ⋁ wyib sl 1

PERUVIAN LACE

Colors A and B

(Multiple of 4 sts)

Cross 4 Wyib sl 4 dropping extra yos, slip these 4 sts back to LH needle, then [k1, p1, k1, p1] into all 4 sts held tog.

Rnd 1 With A, knit.

Rnd 2 With A, purl.

Rnd 3 With B, *k1 wrapping yarn twice around needle; rep from * to end.

Rnd 4 With B, *Cross 4; rep from * to end.

Rnds 5 and 7 With A, knit.

Rnds 6 and 8 With A, purl.

Rnd 9 With A, *k1 wrapping yarn twice around needle; rep from * to end.

Rnd 10 With A, purl dropping extra wraps.

Rep rnds 1–10.

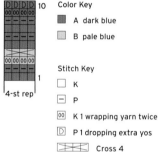

Color Key
- ■ A dark blue
- ■ B pale blue

Stitch Key
- □ K
- ⊟ P
- 00 K 1 wrapping yarn twice
- D P 1 dropping extra yos
- ⊏⊐⊏⊐ Cross 4

WHEN DOVES CRY

Colors A and B

(Multiple of 4 sts)

Tweed st Insert RH needle into next st 2 rows below and pull up loop, k next st on LH needle, pass loop over that st.

Prep rnd With B, knit.

Rnd 1 With A, *k3, Tweed st; rep from * to end.

Rnd 2 With A, knit.

Rnd 3 With B, *k1, Tweed st, k2; rep from * to end.

Rnd 4 With B, knit.

Rep rnds 1–4.

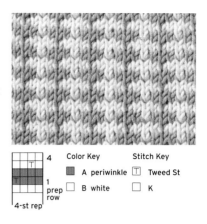

Color Key
■ A periwinkle
□ B white

Stitch Key
T Tweed St
□ K

4-st rep

Slip Stitch Patterns

SLIP STITCH WAFFLE

(Multiple of 5 sts)

Rnd 1 *P1, yo, p4; rep from * to end.

Rnd 2 *Wyib sl 1 dropping the yo of previous rnd, k4; rep from * to end.

Rnds 3, 4, 5 and 6 *Wyib sl 1, k4; rep from * to end.

Rep rnds 1–6.

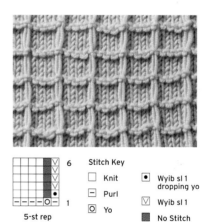

Stitch Key
□ Knit
− Purl
O Yo
• Wyib sl 1 dropping yo
V Wyib sl 1
■ No Stitch

5-st rep

PEAS AND CARROTS

Colors MC, A and B

(Multiple of 4 sts)

Rnd 1 With MC, knit.

Rnds 2 and 3 With A, *k2, wyib sl 2; rep from * to end.

Rnd 4 With MC, knit.

Rnds 5 and 6 With C, *wyib sl 2, k2; rep from * to end.

Rep rnds 1–6.

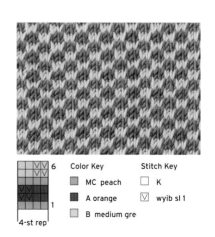

Color Key
■ MC peach
■ A orange
□ B medium gre

Stitch Key
□ K
V wyib sl 1

4-st rep

MASONRY

Colors A and B

(Multiple of 4 sts)

Rnd 1 With A, knit.

Rnd 2 With A, purl.

Rnds 3 and 4 With B, *wyib sl 1, k3; rep from * to end.

Rnds 5 and 6 With A, rep rnds 1 and 2.

Rnds 7 and 8 With B, *k2, wyib sl 1, k1; rep from * to end.

Rep rnds 1–8.

8

Color Key	Stitch Key
☐ A peach	☐ K
■ B rust	⊟ P
	☑ wyib sl 1

1

4-st rep

TINY BROCADE

Colors A and B

(Multiple of 4 sts)

Rnds 1 and 5 With A, knit.

Rnd 2 With B, *wyib sl 1, k1, wyif sl 1, k1; rep from * to end.

Rnd 3 With B, *wyib sl 1, k3; rep from * to end.

Rnd 4 With A, *k2, wyif sl 1, k1; rep from * to end.

Rnd 6 With B, *wyif sl 1, k1, wyib sl 1, k1; rep from * to end.

Rnd 7 With B, *k2, wyib sl 1, k1; rep from * to end.

Rnd 8 With A, *wyib sl 1, k3; rep from * to end.

Rep rnds 1–8.

8

Color Key	Stitch Key
■ A dark green	☐ K
☐ B light green	☑ wyib sl 1
	☑ wyif sl 1

1

4-st rep

LINKS

Colors A and B

(Multiple of 8 sts)

Rnds 1 and 2 With A, knit.

Rnds 3 and 4 With B, wyib sl 1, k5, wyib sl 1, k1; rep from * to end.

Rnds 5 and 6 With A, k1, wyib sl 1, k3, wyib sl 1, k2; rep from * to end.

Rnds 7 and 8 With B, *k2, wyib sl 1, k1, wyib sl 1, k3; rep from * to end.

Rnds 9 and 10 With A, rep rows 5 and 6.

Rnds 11 and 12 With B, rep rows 3 and 4.

Rnds 13 and 14 With A, knit.

Rep rnds 1–14.

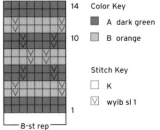

14

10

Color Key
■ A dark green
☐ B orange

Stitch Key
☐ K
☑ wyib sl 1

1

8-st rep

SUCCOTASH

Colors MC, A, B, C and D

(Multiple of 4 sts)

Prep row With MC, knit.

Rnd 1 With A, *k2, [wyib sl 1] twice; rep from * to end.

Rnds 2 and 4 With MC, *[wyib sl 1] twice, k2; rep from * to end.

Rnd 3 With B, *k2, [wyib sl 1] twice; rep from * to end.

Rnd 5 With C, *[wyib sl 1] twice, k2; rep from * to end.

Rnd 6 With MC, *k2, [wyib sl 1] twice; rep from * to end.

Rnd 7 With D, *[wyib sl 1] twice, k2; rep from * to end.

Rnd 8 With MC, rep row 6.

Rep rnds 1–8.

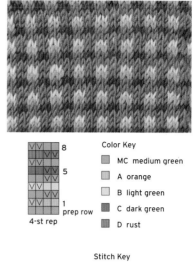

4-st rep

Color Key
- MC medium green
- A orange
- B light green
- C dark green
- D rust

Stitch Key
- ☑ wyib sl 1

Lace Stitches

FAGGOTING

(Multiple of 3 sts)

Rnd 1 *K1, yo, k2tog; rep from * to end.

Rnd 2 *P2tog, yo, p1; rep from * to end.

Rep rnds 1 and 2.

3-st rep

Stitch Key
- ☐ Knit
- ☐ Purl
- ☐ Yo
- ☒ K2tog
- ☒ P2tog

CHEVRON EYELET

(Multiple of 11 sts)

Rnd 1 *K3, k2tog, yo, k1, yo, k2tog tbl, k3; rep from * to end.

Rnd 2 and all even-numbered rnds Knit.

Rnd 3 *K2, k2tog, yo, k3, yo, k2tog tbl, k2; rep from * to end.

Rnd 5 *K1, k2tog, yo, k5, yo, k2tog tbl, k1; rep from * to end.

Rnd 7 *K2tog, yo, k7, yo, k2tog tbl; rep from * to end.

Rnd 8 Knit.

Rep rnds 1–8.

11-st rep

Stitch Key
- ☐ Knit
- ☒ K2tog
- ☐ Yo
- ◺ K2tog tbl

MINI DIAMOND

(Multiple of 8 sts)

Rnd 1 *K1, k2tog, yo, k1, yo, ssk, k2; rep from * to end.

Rnd 2 and all even-numbered rnds Knit.

Rnd 3 *K2tog, yo, k3, yo, ssk, k1; rep from * to end.

Rnd 5 *Yo, k5, yo, SK2P; rep from * to end.

Rnd 7 *Yo, ssk, k3, k2tog, yo, k1; rep from * to end.

Rnd 9 *K1, yo, ssk, k1, k2tog, yo, k2; rep from * to end.

Rnd 11 *K2, yo, SK2P, yo, k3; rep from * to end.

Rnd 12 Knit.

Rep rnds 1–12.

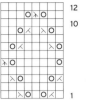

12
10
1

8-st rep

Stitch Key

☐ Knit

Ⓞ Yo

◪ K2tog

◪ Ssk

◪ SK2P

EYELET ZIGZAG

(Multiple of 7 sts)

Rnd 1 *K2, k2tog, yo, k3; rep from * to end.

Rnds 2, 4, 5, 6 and 8 Knit.

Rnd 3 *K1, k2tog, yo, k4; rep from * to end.

Rnd 7 *K3, yo, skp, k2; rep from * to end.

Rnd 9 *K4, yo, skp, k1; rep from * to end.

Rnds 10, 11 and 12 Knit.

Rep rnds 1–12.

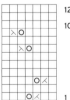

12
10
1

7-st rep

Stitch Key

☐ Knit

Ⓞ Yo

◪ K2tog

◪ Skp

LEAF

(Multiple of 10 sts)

Rnd 1 *K3, yo, k1, yo, k3, SK2P; rep from * to end.

Rnd 2 and all even-numbered rnds Knit.

Rnd 3 *K2, yo, k3, yo, k2, SK2P; rep from * to end.

Rnd 5 *K1, yo, k5, yo, k1, SK2P; rep from * to end.

Rnd 7 *Yo, k7, yo, SK2P; rep from * to end.

Rnd 9 *Yo, k3, SK2P, k3, yo, k1; rep from * to end.

Rnd 11 *K1, yo, k2, SK2P, k2, yo, k2; rep from * to end.

Rnd 13 *K2, yo, k1, SK2P, k1, yo, k3; rep from * to end.

Rnd 15 *K3, yo, SK2P, yo, k4; rep from * to end.

Rnd 16 Knit.

Rep rnds 1–16.

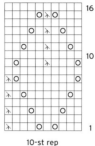

10-st rep

Stitch Key

☐ Knit

◉ Yo

⋏ SK2P

FERN LACE

(Multiple of 10 sts)

Rnds 1 and 9 *K2, yo, k1, yo, k3, S2KP, k1; rep from * to end.

Rnd 2 and all even-numbered rnds Knit.

Rnds 3 and 7 *K1, yo, k1, yo, k3, S2KP, k2; rep from * to end.

Rnd 5 *Yo, k1, yo, k3, S2KP, k3; rep from * to end.

Rnd 11 *K3, yo, k1, yo, k3, S2KP; rep from * to end.

Rnd 12 Knit.

Rep rnds 1–12.

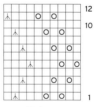

10-st rep

Stitch Key

☐ Knit

◉ Yo

⋏ S2KP

EYELET AND FLAME CHEVRON

(Multiple of 7 sts)

Rnd 1 *Ssk, k5, yo; rep from * to end.

Rnd 2 and all even-numbered rnds Knit.

Rnd 3 *Ssk, k4, yo, k1; rep from * to end.

Rnd 5 *Ssk, k3, yo, k2; rep from * to end.

Rnd 7 *Ssk, k2, yo, k3; rep from * to end.

Rnd 9 *Ssk, k1, yo, k4; rep from * to end.

Rnd 11 *Ssk, yo, k5; rep from * to end.

Rnd 13 *Yo, k5, k2tog; rep from * to end.

Rnd 15 *K1, yo, k4, k2tog; rep from * to end.

Rnd 17 *K2, yo, k3, k2tog; rep from * to end.

Rnd 19 *K3, yo, k2, k2tog; rep from * to end.

Rnd 21 *K4, yo, k1, k2tog; rep from * to end.

Rnd 23 *K5, yo, k2tog; rep from * to end.

Rnd 24 Knit.

Rep rnds 1–24.

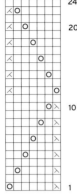

7-st rep

Stitch Key

☐ Knit

Ｏ Yo

◹ K2tog

◺ Ssk

ARROWHEAD LACE

(Multiple of 10 sts)

Rnds 1 and 3 Knit.

Rnd 2 *[Yo, ssk] twice, k1, [k2tog, yo] twice, k1; rep from * to end.

Rnd 4 *K1, yo, ssk, yo, S2KP, yo, k2tog, yo, k2; rep from * to end.

Rep rnds 1–4.

10-st rep

Stitch Key

☐ Knit

Ｏ Yo

◹ K2tog

◺ Ssk

⋏ S2KP

RIPPLE

(Multiple of 18 sts)

Rnd 1 *[K2tog] 3 times, [k1, yo] 6 times, [k2tog] 3 times; rep from * to end.

Rnd 2 Purl.

Rnds 3 and 4 Knit.

Rep rnds 1–4.

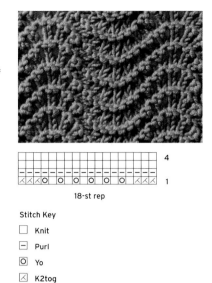

18-st rep

Stitch Key

☐ Knit

⊟ Purl

⊡ Yo

⊠ K2tog

Cables

MINI CABLE

(Multiple of 4 sts)

Rnds 1 and 2 *P1, k3; rep from * to end.

Rnd 3 *P1, skip 2 sts, k third st on LH needle, k first st, k second st, then sl these 3 sts off LH needle; rep from * to end.

Rnd 4 *P1, k3; rep from * to end.

Rep rnds 1–4.

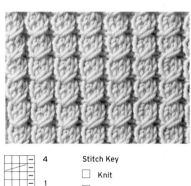

4-st rep

Stitch Key

☐ Knit

⊟ Purl

▱ K 3rd st, then first and 2nd sts

ZIGZAG

(Multiple of 9 sts)

LT With RH needle behind LH needle, skip next st and k the second st tbl, then k skipped st, sl both sts from needle tog.

RT With LH needle behind RH needle, skip next st and k the second st, then k skipped st, sl both sts from needle tog.

Rnd 1 *[LT] 3 times, k3; rep from * to end.

Rnd 2 and all even-numbered rnds Knit.

Rnd 3 *K1, [LT] 3 times, k2; rep from * to end.

Rnd 5 *K2, [LT] 3 times, k1; rep from * to end.

Rnd 7 *K3, [LT] 3 times; rep from * to end.

Rnd 9 *K3, [RT] 3 times; rep from * to end.

Rnd 11 *K2, [RT] 3 times, k1; rep from * to end.

Rnd 13 *K1, [RT] 3 times, k2; rep from * to end.

Rnd 15 *[RT] 3 times, k3; rep from * to end.

Rnd 16 Knit.

Rep rnds 1–16.

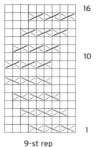

WRAP MOCK CABLE

(Multiple of 4 sts)

MC Sl 1, k2, pass sl st over k2.

Preparation rnd *P1, k3; rep from * to end.

Rnd 1 *P1, MC; rep from * to end.

Rnd 2 *P1, k1, yo, k1; rep from * to end.

Rnds 3 and 4 *P1, k3; rep from * to end.

Rnd 5 and 6 Rep rnds 1 and 2.

Rep rnds 1–6

CHUNKY CABLE RIB

(Multiple of 7 sts)

6-st LC Sl next 3 sts to cn and hold to front, k3, k3 from cn.

Rnds 1 and 2 *K6, p1; rep from * to end.

Rnd 3 *6-st LC, p1; rep from * to end.

Rnds 4, 5, 6, 7 and 8 *K6, p1; rep from * to end.

Rep rnds 1–8.

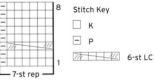

Stitch Key
□ K
⊟ P
◩ 6-st LC

ICE STORM

(Multiple of 6 sts)

4-st RC (right cross) Sl 2 sts to cn and hold to back, k2, k2 from cn.

Rnds 1, 2 and 3 Knit.

Rnd 4 *P2, k4; rep from * to end.

Rnd 5 *P2, 4-st RC; rep from * to end.

Rnd 6 Knit.

Rep rnds 1–6.

Stitch Key
□ K
⊟ P
◪ 4-st RC

WINDSWEPT

(Multiple of 5 sts)

4-st LC (left cross) Sl 2 sts to cn and hold to front, k2, k2 from cn.

Rnds 1 and 2 *P1, k4; rep from * to end.

Rnd 3 *P1, 4-st LC; rep from * to end.

Rnd 4 Rep rnd 1.

Rep rnds 1–4.

Stitch Key
□ K
⊟ P
◩ 4-st LC

FIREFLY

(Multiple of 10 sts)

4-st RC Sl 2 sts to cn and hold to back, k2, k2 from cn.

Rnds 1 and 2 *P1, k4; rep from * to end.

Rnd 3 *P1, 4-st RC, p1, k4; rep from * to end.

Rnds 4-10 Rep rnd 1.

Rnd 11 *P1, k4, p1, 4-st RC; rep from * to end.

Rnds 12, 13 and 14 Rep rnd 1.

Rnd 15 Rep rnd 11.

Rnds 16-22 Rep rnd 1.

Rnd 23 *P1, 4-st RC, p1, k4; rep from * to end.

Rnd 24 Rep rnd 1.

Rep rnds 1–24.

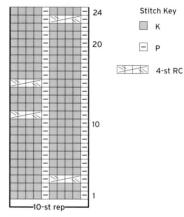

Stitch Key

- ▨ K
- — P
- ⤬⤬ 4-st RC

SMALL CABLE AND EYELET

(Multiple of 11 sts)

4-st RC Sl 2 sts to cn and hold to back, k2, k2 from cn.

Rnds 1 and 3 *P2, k3, p2, k4; rep from * to end.

Rnd 2 *P2, yo, ssk, k1, p2, 4-st RC; rep from * to end.

Rnd 4 *P2, k1, k2tog, yo, p2, k4; rep from * to end.

Rep rnds 1–4.

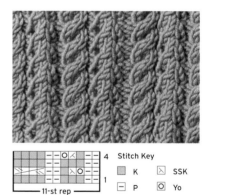

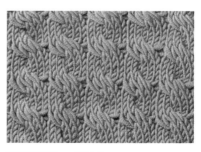

Stitch Key

- ▨ K   ◩ SSK
- — P   O Yo
- ⌧ K2tog   ⤬⤬ 4-st RC

DROPPED-STITCH CABLE

(Multiple of 6 sts)

6-st LPC Sl 3 sts to cn letting extra loops drop, hold to front of work, k3, letting extra loops drop, k3 from cn.

Rnds 1-4 Knit.

Rnd 5 *K next st wrapping yarn twice around needle; rep from * to end.

Rnd 6 *6-st LPC; rep from * to end.

Rep rnds 1–6.

Stitch Key

- ▨ K
- 00 K wrapping yarn twice around needle
- ⤬⤬ 6-st LPC

ACORNS

(Multiple of 8 sts)

RT K2tog, leave sts on LH neeedle, insert RH needle from front between the 2 sts just knit tog and knit the first st again. Sl both sts to RH needle tog.

LT With RH needle behind LH needle, skip one st and k the second st tbl, then insert RH needle into the backs of both sts and k2tog tbl.

Rnds 1 and 7 *K1, p2, k2, p2, k1; rep from * to end.

Rnd 2 *K1, p1, RT, LT, p1, k1; rep from * to end.

Row 3 *K1, p1, k1, p2, k1, p1, k1; rep from * to end.

Row 4 *K1, RT, p2, LT, k1; rep from * to end.

Row 5 *K2, p4, k2; rep from * to end.

Row 6 Knit.

Row 8 *LT, p1, k2, p1, RT; rep from * to end.

Row 9 *P1, k1, p1, k2, p1, k1, p1; rep from * to end.

Row 10 *P1, LT, k2, RT, p1; rep from * to end.

Row 11 *P2, k4, p2; rep from * to end.

Row 12 Knit.

Rep rows 1–12.

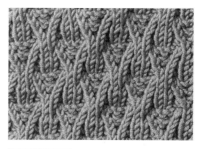

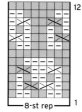

12

Stitch Key

☐ K on RS, p on WS

⊟ P on RS, k on WS

⧖ 2-st RT

⧗ 2-st LT

8-st rep

1

Color

SNOW BERRIES

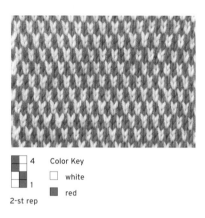

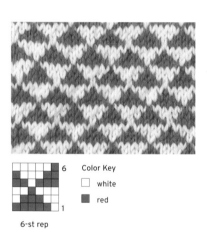 4
1

2-st rep

Color Key
☐ white
■ red

BLUE BIAS

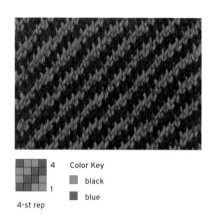

4
1

4-st rep

Color Key
■ black
■ blue

POSEIDON

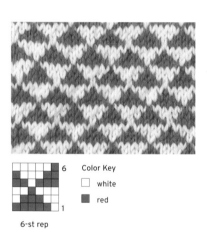

6
1

6-st rep

Color Key
☐ white
■ red

CHECKERED PAST

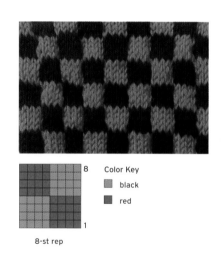

8
1

8-st rep

Color Key
■ black
■ red

HOUNDSTOOTH

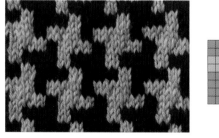

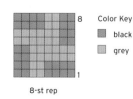 8
1

8-st rep

Color Key
■ black
■ grey

CHAIN-LINK FENCE

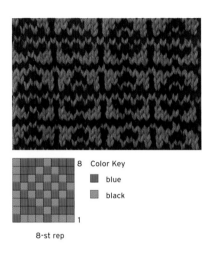

8

Color Key

■ blue

■ black

1

8-st rep

INTO THE WOODS

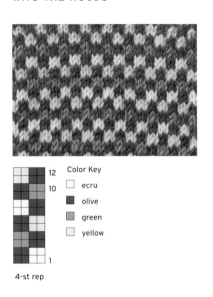

12

10

Color Key

□ ecru

■ olive

■ green

□ yellow

1

4-st rep

EAGLE'S VIEW

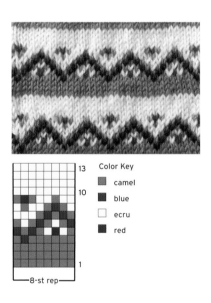

13

10

Color Key

■ camel

■ blue

□ ecru

■ red

1

8-st rep

VIOLETS

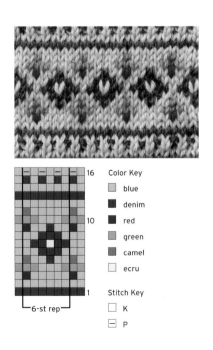

16

10

Color Key

■ blue

■ denim

■ red

■ green

■ camel

□ ecru

Stitch Key

□ K

⊟ P

1

6-st rep

Chapter 6
Sock Knitting Traditions Around the World

Socks are the most humble of clothing items, yet generations of knitters have turned socks into folk art. The threads that run through the years and unite all knitters consist of color and form, intricate designs created and cherished by anonymous knitters with no art training. Yet what they create is truly art—folk art.

Many of the motifs common in folk traditions come directly from nature: animals, birds, flowers, snowflakes, trees. Other geometric shapes come from creative minds that found knitting a fertile field in which to stretch their imaginations.

Though other clothing items may have by necessity been heavy and dark, when it came to socks a riot of color was traditional. Motifs were often exclusive to a geographical area, as were color favorites. Knitters rarely wrote down these patterns. Instead they handed them down as heirlooms from generation to generation. Certain families specialized in particular designs.

Long, cold, dark nights provided plenty of time for knitting socks, which became not only a necessity for warmth and comfort, but objects of great beauty requiring skill and dedication to knit. The socks in this chapter take their inspiration from those long-ago knitters, and by knitting them, you will continue to pass on the thread that unites the world's sock knitters.

Fair Isle

Fair Isle is the most remote of the Shetland Islands, located off the northern coast of Scotland. On this tiny island a knitting tradition developed that has endured for centuries.

Colorful bands of geometric designs form the basis for Fair Isle work, and although an overall design may contain many colors, only two are ever used in one row. In the method for carrying the yarn, called stranding, the color not in use is carried across the back of the work, leaving "floats." Tension of the floating yarn is very important: if it is carried too tightly, the work will draw in; if it is too loose, the floats will catch when the item is worn.

On the island, patterns have been handed down from generation to generation, and are usually carried in the minds of the knitters, not written down. Today most Fair Isle patterns are reproduced in charts. Fair Isle is traditionally worked in the round, as yokes for sweaters, as berets, and as socks and mittens.

The Patterns section includes two Fair Isle–inspired sock patterns: the Nordic Star adult socks (page 122) and the Toddler Socks (page 126). Both are modern adaptations using traditional Fair Isle two-color patterns in nontraditional colors and combinations.

Bavaria

Bavaria, a region in southern Germany adjacent to Austria, is known for a rich knitting tradition characterized by an endless variety of traveling twisted stitches. These wonderful stitches twist and turn and interlace themselves, giving a lovely understated texture to the work. The twisted stitches are worked by knitting or purling into the backs of stitches, which creates a highly embossed design, usually on a purled background. Cable needles are sometimes, but not always, used to work the cross-overs. The overall designs are created with many narrow bands of motifs arranged side by side.

Knitting from the Tyrolean region is quite different, often using an overall small motif worked in two colors. Bands of multicolor patterning, featuring leaf and flower designs or other motifs from nature, are often used as borders.

The Bavarian knitting tradition is represented here by a pair of Bavarian Socks (page 13o) that incorporate traditional traveling twist-stitch patterns.

Latvia

This small country on the Baltic Sea is a nation of knitters. When the NATO summit meeting was held in Latvia in 2006, the country's knitters fell to work and knitted 4,500 pairs of traditional colorful mittens so that each official attending could take home a pair.

Latvian knitting shares some of the colorful traditions of intricate geometric patterning with its neighbor, Estonia. Hundreds of traditional motifs with bold and bright colorways are passed down from generation to generation. Each region of the country has its own specific motifs imbued with deep meaning for the locals. Allover patterning is common.

Specialty techniques such as a twisted cast-on, herringbone braids and scalloped edges set the work apart. The region is represented in this book by Lizbeth Upitis's Latvian Socks (page 133), which incorporate both the openwork and two-color knitting traditions.

Estonia

Estonia is another small country on the Baltic Sea with a big knitting tradition. Its colorful repeat patterns include some that have been in continuous use since the sixteenth century. Estonia is bordered on the south by Latvia, with which it shares some knitting traditions, and on the east by Russia.

Children, both boys and girls, learn to knit early in school, and most wardrobes include collections of hand-knitted socks and mittens. More than 200 traditional knitting patterns are in use today, many connected to nature.

Candace Eisner-Strick's Bavarian Socks use the traditional twisted stitch technique.

Lizbeth Upitis incorporated geometric patterning, lace and texture interest into her interpretation of Latvian knitting traditions.

Animals are featured, with favorites such as pole-cat-paws, swallowtail and elk-antler. As in most Nordic countries, the long, cold, dark winter months seem to bring out the desire for color in knitting.

Estonia also has a strong tradition of knitted lace, which combines openwork and texture. The texture comes from use of *nupps*, which are a sort of bobble. These rounded dimensional bumps are arranged in a variety of ways and feature the traditional lily-of-the-valley design. Yarn overs, decreases and nupps are artfully worked into exquisite knitted laces. The Estonian Socks on page 138 were inspired by a pair of antique socks patterned with diamonds and zigzag lines.

Scandinavia

Ski sweaters first brought knitting in Scandinavia to the attention of the rest of the world. But there's more to knitting in Scandinavia than sweaters. Bold motifs such as geometrics, deer, foxes, snowflakes, hearts and flowers abound—all the many symbols of the natural world. Vibrant colorways, particularly graphic designs in red, white and black, can be found in most of the region's knitting. Priscilla Gibson-Roberts's Scandinavian Socks (page 142) use this traditional color combination and motifs in a very nontraditional way—to create a pair that coordinate but do not match exactly.

Turkey

Turkey, with borders on both the Aegean and the Mediterranean Seas, has a long tradition of knitting. Turkey's knitters favor an unusual combination of forceful design with bold colors.

Mari Lynn Patrick combined Turkish motifs with western shapings in these colorful socks.

The traditional geometric motifs have a unique look because the grounds and the motifs are given equal color importance, instead of the grounds receding. Grounds are often striped, which sets off the motifs with a distinctive look. The traditional Turkish sock toe has a pointed toe and heel and is often accented with a tassel.

The poetic symbolism of Turkish patterns in sock knitting originated more than 2,000 years ago and is reinterpreted here by Mari Lynn Patrick (page 146). The chart symbols shown as "v" on the color charts are the pattern repetitions that convey some of this symbolism. These socks have both the *cengel* symbol for hook, representing a hook to hold onto a lover's heart, and a gridwork symbol which is interpreted in a multicolor way. The gridwork is a cultural symbol for the wood grids that are fitted over house windows and that allow women to see the outside world without being seen. Combining the two symbols is a way to portray two of the deep mysteries of the feminine soul.

Patterns

In the following pages, we present a variety of sock patterns for knitters of all skill levels, the great majority newly commissioned for this book. There are simple patterns appropriate for those of you who have never knitted a sock before, and there are patterns that require advanced knitting techniques to challenge and delight the most experienced sock knitter. There are plain, basic patterns and patterns with truly fabulous embellishments. There are patterns written for toe-up and top-down construction as well as patterns written for double-pointed needles or circular needles (use the table on page 81 to find exactly what you're looking for).

No matter the style, if it can fit a foot, you'll find it here, starting with a simple tube sock that requires no heel shaping (page 82) and ending with a lavishly embroidered sock that is cast on at the ankle and worked both up and down (page 166). In between, you'll find the simplest of toe-up socks (page 84); a family of basic socks for men, women and children (page 89); "sockies" that you can make using leftover yarn (page 99); Cat Bordhi's Flow Motion socks, with her own explanation of the Magic Loop two-circular method; and fabulous new patterns that interpret the Fair Isles, Scandinavian, Bavarian, Latvian, Estonian and Turkish knitting traditions.

Sock Techniques Chart

Pattern	Technique	Needles Used
Cabled Top Socks (page 82)	Top down	Double-pointed
Toe-Up Socks (page 84)	Toe up	Double-pointed
Anklets (page 86)	Toe up	Double-pointed
Ribbed Socks (page 89)	Top down	Double-pointed
Mosaic Socks (page 92)	Top down	Double-pointed
Garter Heel Socks (page 96)	Top down	Double-pointed
Sockies (page 99)	Toe up	Double-pointed
Renaissance Socks (page 101)	Top down	Double-pointed
Zigzag Socks (page 104)	Top down	Double-pointed
Leaf Lace Socks (page 107)	Top down	Double-pointed
Diamond Lace Socks (page 110)	Toe up	Double-pointed
Flow Motion Socks (page 113)	Toe up	Two circulars
Ornate Socks (page 118)	Top down	Two circulars
Nordic Star Socks (page 122)	Top down	Double-pointed
Toddler Socks (page 126)	Top down	Double-pointed
Bavarian Socks (page 130)	Top down	Two circulars
Latvian Socks (page 133)	Top down	Two circulars
Estonian Socks (page 138)	Top down	Double-pointed
Scandinavian Socks (page 142)	Toe up	Double-pointed
Turkish Socks (page 146)	Top down	Double-pointed, straight
Color Wheel Socks (page 150)	Toe up	Double-pointed
Arched Shaped Socks (page 154)	Top down	Double-pointed
Man's Classic Argyles (page 158)	Top down	Double-pointed, straight
Embroidered Stockings (page 162)	Toe up	Double-pointed
Embroidered Socks (page 166)	Up and down from ankle	Double-pointed

FINISHED MEASUREMENTS

Approx 15½"/40cm from cuff to toe

MATERIALS

1 3½ oz/100g ball (approx 459yd/420m) Schoeller & Stahl/Skacel Collection Inc. **Fortissima Colori** (wool/nylon) in #9094 marine

One set (5) dpns size 3 (3.25mm) OR SIZE TO OBTAIN GAUGE

One crochet hook size Q (15mm)

GAUGE

30 sts and 42 rows = 4"/10cm over St st using size 3 (3.25mm) needles.

TAKE TIME TO CHECK GAUGE.

Cabled Top Socks

by Noreen Crone-Findlay

This tube sock has chained I-cord at the cuff and a pointed toe. It is a single tube sock with no heel shaping.

CUFF

Cable edge

Cast on 3 sts. Work in I-cord (see page 172) for 55"/140cm. Bind off. With I-cord and crochet hook, make a slipknot and chain 15 to measure approx 10½"/26.5cm. Fasten off and sew cast-on end of chain to bound-off end to form cuff.

LEG

Working across one edge of I-cord chain, pick up and k 57 sts evenly around. Divide sts evenly over 3 needles. Place marker for end of rnd and sl marker every rnd.

Stitch pat

Note

The extra stitch causes this simple rib pat to spiral.

Rnd 1 *K6, p2; rep from * until leg measures 13"/33cm or 2½"/6.5cm from desired length.

TOE

Rnd 1 *K2tog, k17; rep from * to end—54 sts.
Rnd 2 For Needle 1, *k1, skp, k to last 3 sts, k2tog, k1; rep from * for Needles 2 and 3.
Rnds 3 and 4 Knit.
Rep rnds 2–4 until there are 12 sts.
Break yarn leaving a 6"/15cm tail. Thread tail through rem sts twice, pull tightly and secure.

FINISHED MEASUREMENTS

6"/15cm from cuff to heel

Approx 9½"/24cm from heel to toe

MATERIALS

2 2oz/57g balls (each approx 215yd/197m) Lorna's Laces **Shepherd Sock** (wool/nylon) in tuscany

One set (5) dpns size 1 (2.25mm) OR SIZE TO OBTAIN GAUGE

GAUGE

28 sts and 40 rnds = 4"/10cm over St st using size 1 (2.25mm) needles.

TAKE TIME TO CHECK GAUGE.

Toe-Up Socks

by Amy Swenson

This sock is knit from the toe up with short-row heel

and toe and k1, p1 ribbed instep and leg.

TOE

Using provisional crochet cast-on, cast on 29 sts.

Row 1 (WS) Purl.

Row 2 K to last st, WT.

Row 3 P to last st, WT.

Row 4 K to 1 st before last wrapped st, WT.

Row 5 P to 1 st before last wrapped st, WT.

Rep rows 4 and 5 until there are 11 sts between wrapped sts.

Next row K to next wrapped st, WW, WT.

Next row P to next wrapped st, WW, WT.

Rep last 2 rows until all sts have been worked, omitting WT at ends of last 2 rows.

FOOT

Carefully remove waste yarn and slip 29 sts evenly over 2 dpns, divide rem 29 sts over 2 dpns—58 sts. Place marker for end of rnd.

Rnd 1 K29 sole sts, [p1, k1] 14 times, p1.

Rep rnd 1 until foot measures 7½"/19cm or 2"/5cm from desired length.

HEEL

Work same as toe, starting with row 2 over 29 sole sts.

LEG

With RS facing, k29, pickup and k2 in corner of heel, [p1, k1] 14 times, p1, pick up and k2 in corner of heel—62 sts.

Dec rnd 1 K29, skp, rib 29, k2tog.

Dec rnd 2 K28, skp, rib 28, k2tog—58 sts.

Pat rnd *K1, p1; rep from * to end.

Rep pat rnd until leg measures 7"/18cm or desired length from top of heel.

Bind off loosely in rib.

FINISHED MEASUREMENTS

4"/10cm from cuff to heel

Approx 10½"/26cm from heel to toe

MATERIALS

1 4½ oz/128g ball (approx 360yd/329m) Blue Moon
Fiber Arts **Socks That Rock Lightweight** (wool)
in farmhouse
One set (5) dpns size 2 (2.75mm) OR SIZE TO
OBTAIN GAUGE

GAUGE

30 sts and 44 rnds = 4"/10cm over St st using size 2
(2.5mm) needles.
TAKE TIME TO CHECK GAUGE.

Anklets

by Christine Walter

This anklet is knit from the toe up with side-increased toe, short-row heel worked with yarn overs and a short ribbed cuff. A picot bind-off is used for a stretchy opening.

M1L (Left slanting inc) With LH needle, lift strand between needles from front to back and k tbl.
M1R (Right slanting inc) With LH needle, lift strand between needles from back to front and k.

ssp [Sl 1 knitwise] twice, p2tog tbl.
sssp [Sl 1 knitwise] 3 times, p3tog tbl.

TOE

Using single cast-on (see Techniques), cast on 4 sts.
Row 1 Kfb of each st—8 sts.
Row 2 *K1, sl 1 wyif; rep from * to end.
Remove needle (knitting will separate into two sides) and slip a dpn through the 4 sts on each side. K2 and pm for end of rnd.

Toe shaping

Rnd 1 For Needle 1, k1, M1R, k1. For Needle 2, k1, M1L, k1. For Needle 3, k1, M1R, k1. For Needle 4, k1, M1L.
Rnd 2 *For Needle 1, k to last st, M1R, k1. For Needle 2, k1, M1L, k to end. Rep from * for Needles 3 and 4.
Rep rnd 2 until there are 32 (36) sts.
Next rnd Knit.
Rep last 2 rnds until there are 60 (64) sts.

FOOT

Work even in St st until foot measures 7 (8)"/18 (20.5)cm or 2"/5cm less than desired length.

HEEL

Worked over 30 (32) sts on Needles 1 and 4.

Row 1 (RS) Cont with Needle 4, k to last st on Needle 1, turn—30 (32) sts on one needle.

Row 2 Yo wyib, p to last st, turn.

Row 3 Yo wyif, k to 1 st before last yo, turn.

Rep Rows 2 and 3 until there are 11 (13) sts between yos, ending with row 2.

Next row Yo wyif, k to next yo, sl yo knitwise and sl back onto LH needle, k2tog, turn.

Next row Yo wyib, p to next yo, ssp, turn.

Next row Yo wyif, k to next yo, [sl yo knitwise] twice and sl both sts back onto LH needle, k3tog, turn.

Next row Yo wyib, p to next yo, sssp, turn.

Rep last 2 rows until all yos have been worked, working **last RS row** Yo wyif, k15 (16)—30 (32) sts plus 1 yo at each end. Pm for end of rnd.

LEG

For Needle 1, k to yo, sl yo knitwise then sl yo onto Needle 2. For Needle 2, k2tog (yo plus next st), k to end. For Needle 3, k to last st, sl yo on Needle 4 knitwise then sl yo onto Needle 3, ssk (next st plus yo). For Needle 4, k to end—60 (64) sts.

Work even in St st for 1"/2.5cm, then work in k2, p2 rib for 2 (2¾)"/5 (7)cm.

Picot bind-off

Bind off 1, *bind off 2 sts, cast on 2 sts using cable cast-on (see page 26), turn, pass 2nd and first sts over last st, bind off 2 sts; rep from *, end last rep bind off 1 st. Fasten off. Each picot sits between the 2 purl sts of k2, p2 rib.

SIZES

Instructions are written for man's 9½ to 12, woman's 8½ to 10½ and child's 6 to 7½.

FINISHED MEASUREMENTS

Leg circumference 8 (7½, 6¼)"/20.5 (19, 16)cm

Foot length 8½ (7½, 5¼)"/21.5 (19, 13.5)cm

MATERIALS

3 1¾oz/50g balls (each approx 215yds/197m) of Brown Sheep Company **Wildfoote Luxury** (wool/nylon) in #SY08 geranium for man's, 2 in #SY41 dark caramel for woman's, or 2 in #SY03 brilliant bouquet for child's.

One set (4) dpns size 1 (2.25mm) OR SIZE TO OBTAIN GAUGE

Ribbed Socks

These socks, worked from the top down with heel flaps and wedge toes, are a wardrobe staple for the whole family. This is a vintage Vogue *pattern.*

Stitch markers

GAUGE

32 sts and 44 rnds to 4"/10cm over St st using size 1 (2.25mm) needles.

TAKE TIME TO CHECK GAUGE.

MAN'S SOCKS

CUFF
Cast on 64 sts loosely and divide evenly over 3 needles. Join, taking care not to twist sts. Place marker for end of rnd and sl marker every rnd. Work in k1, p1 rib for 3"/7.5cm, inc 8 sts evenly spaced across last rnd—72 sts.

LEG
Rnd 1 K2, *p2, k4; rep from * around, end p2, k2.
Rep rnd 1 until leg measures 6"/15cm from beg.
Next rnd With Needles 1 and 2, work in pat; with Needle 3, work 4 sts. Sl rem 20 sts onto a spare dpn, then sl first 20 sts from Needle 1 onto same spare dpn—40 sts for heel flap. Divide rem 32 sts onto 2 needles for instep to be worked later.

HEEL
Heel flap
Heel flap is worked back and forth over these 40 sts.
Dec row K7, [k2tog, k6] 4 times, k1—36 sts.
Row 1 (WS) Sl 1, purl to end.
Row 2 *Sl 1, k1; rep from * to end.
Rep rows 1 and 2 until there are 34 rows in heel flap.

Turn heel
Row 1 (WS) Sl 1, p20, p2tog, p1, turn.
Row 2 Sl 1, k7, ssk, k1, turn.
Row 3 Sl 1, p to 1 st before gap, p2tog, p1, turn.
Row 4 Sl 1, k to 1 st before gap, ssk, k1, turn.
Rep rows 3 and 4 until all heel sts have been worked—22 sts. Do not turn on last row.

GUSSETS
Cont with same needle (Needle 1), pick up and k18 sts along side of heel flap; with needle 2, work 32 instep sts keeping pat as established; with Needle 3, pick up and k18 sts along other side of heel flap and k11 from Needle 1—90 sts total, 29 sts each on Needles 1 and 3, 32 sts on Needle 2. Place marker for end of rnd.
Shape gussets
Rnd 1 Work even in pats as est.

Rnd 2 For Needle 1, k to last 3 sts, k2tog, k1; for Needle 2, work even in pat; for Needle 3, k1, ssk, k to end.
Rep rnds 1 and 2 until there are 72 sts.

FOOT
Work even in pats as est until foot measures 6½"/16.5cm or until 2"/5cm less than desired finished length.

TOE
Discontinue instep pat. Redistribute sts as foll: 18 sts on each of Needles 3 and 1, and 36 sts on Needle 2.
Rnd 1 Knit.
Rnd 2 For Needle 1, k to last 3 sts, k2tog, k1; for Needle 2, k1, ssk, k to last 3 sts, k2tog, k1; for Needle 3, k1, ssk, k to end.
Rep rnds 1 and 2 until there are 20 sts rem. With Needle 3, k5 from Needle 1.
Graft toe sts using Kitchener st (see page 33).

WOMAN'S SOCKS

CUFF
Cast on 66 sts loosely and divide evenly over 3 needles. Join, taking care not to twist sts. Place marker for end of rnd and sl marker every rnd. Work in k1, p1 rib for 2"/5cm.

LEG
Rnd 1 K1, *p2, k4; rep from *, end p2, k3.
Rep rnd 1 until leg measures 3"/7.5cm from beg. Work first 32 sts and distribute evenly over 2 needles for instep to be worked later. [K10, k2tog] twice, k10—32 sts on one needle for heel flap.

HEEL
Heel flap is worked back and forth over 32 sts.
Row 1 (WS) Sl 1, p to end.
Row 2 *Sl 1, k1; rep from * to end.
Rep rows 1 and 2 until there are 32 rows in heel flap.
Turn heel
Row 1 (WS) Sl 1, p18, p2tog, p1, turn.

Row 2 Sl 1, k7, ssk, k1, turn.

Row 3 Sl 1, p to 1 st before gap, p2tog, p1, turn.

Row 4 Sl 1, k to 1 st before gap, ssk, k1, turn.

Rep rows 3 and 4 until all heel sts have been worked—20 sts.

GUSSETS

With same needle (Needle 1), pick up and k17 sts along side of heel flap; with Needle 2, cont in pat on 32 instep sts; with Needle 3, pick up and k17 sts along other side of heel flap, k10 from Needle 1—86 sts. Place marker for end of rnd.

Shape gussets

Rnd 1 Knit.

Rnd 2 For Needle 1, k to last 3 sts, k2tog, k1; for Needle 2, work in pat; for Needle 3, k1, ssk, k to end.

Rep rnds 1 and 2 until there are 64 sts.

FOOT

Cont in pats as est until foot measures 5¾"/14.5cm or 1¾"/4.5cm less than desired length.

TOE

Rnd 1 Knit.

Rnd 2 For Needle 1, k to last 3 sts, k2tog, k1; for Needle 2, k1, ssk, k to last 3 sts, k2tog, k1; for Needle 3, k1, ssk, k to end.

Rep rnds 1 and 2 until there are 16 sts. With Needle 3, k4 from Needle 1.

Graft toe sts using Kitchener st (see page 33).

CHILD'S SOCKS

CUFF

Cast on 56 sts loosely, divide over 3 needles as foll: Needle 1—14 sts, Needle 2—29 sts, Needle 3—13 sts. Join, taking care not to twist sts. Place marker for end of rnd and sl marker every rnd. Work in k1, p1 rib for 1½"/4cm.

LEG

Rnd 1 *K3, p1; rep from * around.

Rep rnd 1 until leg measures 4"/10cm from beg, work ssk at end of last rnd—55 sts.

HEEL

Heel flap

Heel flap is worked back and forth over 26 sts. Divide sts on Needle 2 over 2 needles for instep to be worked later; with Needle 3, k13 from Needle 1—26 sts on one needle.

Row 1 (WS) Sl 1, p to end.

Row 2 *Sl 1, k1; rep from * to end.

Rep rows 1 and 2 until there are 28 rows in heel flap.

Turn heel

Row 1 (WS) Sl 1, p14, p2tog, p1, turn.

Row 2 Sl 1, k5, ssk, k1, turn.

Row 3 Sl 1, p to 1 st before gap, p2tog, p1, turn.

Row 4 Sl 1, k to 1 st before gap, ssk, k1, turn.

Rep rows 3 and 4 until all heel flap sts have been worked—16 sts.

GUSSETS

With same needle (Needle 1), pick up and k15 sts along side of heel flap, with Needle 2, work in pat across 29 instep sts, with Needle 3, pick up and k15 sts along other side of heel flap and k8 from Needle 1—75 sts. Place marker for end of rnd.

Shape gussets

Rnd 1 For Needle 1, k to last 3 sts, k2tog, k1; for Needle 2, work in pat; for Needle 3, k1, ssk, k to end.

Rnd 2 Work in pats as est.

Rep rnds 1 and 2 until there are 57 sts.

FOOT

Work even until foot measures 3¾"/9.5cm or 1½"/4cm less than desired finished length.

Next rnd K28, k2tog, k27—56 sts.

TOE

Rnd 1 Knit.

Rnd 2 For Needle 1, k to last 3 sts, k2tog, k1; for Needle 2, k1, ssk, k to last 3 sts, k2tog, k1; for Needle 3, k1, ssk, k to end.

Rep rnds 1 and 2 until there are 16 sts. With Needle 3, k4 from Needle 1.

Graft toe sts using Kitchener st (see page 33).

FINISHED MEASUREMENTS

2½"/6.5cm from cuff to heel (folded)

Approx 9½"/24cm from heel to toe

MATERIALS

2 1¾ oz/50g skeins (each approx 175yd/160m)
Koigu Wool Designs **KPPPM** (wool) in #P212 berry multi
(MC)

1 skein each #2235DG grape (A) and #2235
raspberry (B)

One set (5) dpns size 2 (2.75mm) OR SIZE TO
OBTAIN GAUGE

GAUGE

30 sts and 44 rnds = 4"/10cm over St st using size 2
(2.5mm) needles.

TAKE TIME TO CHECK GAUGE.

Note

Always slip stitches with yarn in back on right-side rows
and with yarn in front on wrong side rows. Carry yarn
loosely behind unworked stitches.

Mosaic Socks

by Christine Walter

This anklet is knit from the cuff down with

a mosaic fold-down cuff, flap heel and star toe.

Pattern Stitch

Mosaic floral band (multiple of 8 sts)

Rnd 1 With B, *sl 1, k3; rep from * to end.

Rnd 2 With B, *sl 1, p3; rep from * to end.

Rnd 3 With A, *k1, sl 1; rep from * to end.

Rnd 4 With A, *p1, sl 1; rep from * to end.

Rnd 5 With B, *sl 1, k7; rep from * to end.

Rnd 6 With B, *sl 1, p7; rep from * to end.

Rnd 7 With A, *k3, sl 3, k2; rep from * to end.

Rnd 8 With A, *p3, sl 3, p2; rep from * to end.

Rnd 9 With B, *sl 1, k6, sl 1; rep from * to end.

Rnd 10 With B, *sl 1, p6, sl 1; rep from * to end.

Rnd 11 With A, *[k1, sl 1] twice, k2, sl 1, k1; rep
from * to end.

Rnd 12 With A, *[p1, sl 1] twice, p2, sl 1, p1; rep
from * to end.

Rnd 13 With B, *sl 1, k3, sl 2, k2; rep from *
to end.

Rnd 14 With B, *sl 1, p3, sl 2, p2; rep from *
to end.

Rnd 15 With A, *k7, sl 1; rep from * to end.

Rnd 16 With A, *p7, sl 1; rep from * to end.

Rnd 17 With B, knit.

Rnd 18 With B, purl.

Rnd 19 With A, *k3, sl 1, k4; rep from * to end.

Rnd 20 With A, *p3, sl 1, p4; rep from * to end.

Rnd 21 With B, *sl 2, k2, sl 1, k3; rep from *
to end.

Mosaic Floral Band

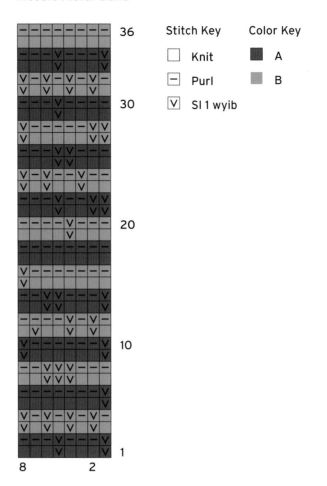

Stitch Key

☐ Knit

⊟ Purl

Ⅴ Sl 1 wyib

Color Key

⬛ A

⬜ B

Rnd 22 With B, *sl 2, k2, sl 1, p3; rep from * to end.

Rnd 23 With A, *[k2, sl 1] twice, k1, sl 1; rep from * to end.

Rnd 24 With A, *[p2, sl 1] twice, p1, sl 1; rep from * to end.

Rnd 25 With B, *k3, sl 2, k3; rep from * to end.

Rnd 26 With B, *p3, sl 2, p3; rep from * to end.

Rnd 27 With A, *sl 2, k5, sl 1; rep from * to end.

Rnd 28 With A, *sl 2, p5, sl 1; rep from * to end.

Rnd 29 With B, *k4, sl 1, k3; rep from * to end.

Rnd 30 With B, *k4, sl 1, p3; rep from * to end.

Rnd 31 With A, *k1, sl 1; rep from * to end.

Rnd 32 With A, *p1, sl 1; rep from * to end.

Rnd 33 With B, *sl 1, k3; rep from * to end.

Rnd 34 With B, *sl 1, p3; rep from * to end.

Rnd 35 With A, knit.

Rnd 36 With A, purl.

CUFF

With A, cast on 64 sts. Divide sts evenly over 4 needles. Join, taking care not to twist sts. Place marker for end of rnd and sl marker every rnd. K 1 rnd, p 1 rnd. Work 36 rnds of Mosaic Floral Band for cuff, breaking off B after rnd 34. With A, p 2 rnds.

Invert knitting by flipping RS of cuff to inside and reverse direction of knitting. K 1 rnd, then work in k1, p1 rib for 16 rnds. Break off A. With MC, work in St st for 10 rnds. Transfer sts from 2nd needle onto first needle for heel—32 sts.

HEEL
Heel flap
Worked over 32 sts.

Row 1 (RS) *Sl 1, k1; rep from * to end, turn.

Row 2 Sl 1, p to end, turn.

Rep rows 1 and 2 until there are 30 rows in heel flap.

Turn heel
Row 1 (RS) Sl 1, k18, ssk, k1, turn.

Row 2 Sl 1, p5, p2tog, p1, turn.

Row 3 Sl 1, k to 1 st before gap, ssk, k1, turn.

Row 4 Sl 1, p to 1 st before gap, p2tog, p1, turn.

Rep rows 3 and 4 until all heel sts have been worked—20 sts.

GUSSETS
With RS facing and spare needle, k9. For Needle 1, k9 then pick up and k16 sts along side of heel flap; for Needles 2 and 3, k32; for Needle 4, pick up and k16 sts along side of heel flap, then k9 from spare needle—82 sts. Pm for end of rnd.

Shape gussets
Rnd 1 For Needle 1, k to last 3 sts, k2tog, k1. For Needles 2 and 3, knit. For Needle 4, k1, ssk, k to end.

Rnd 2 Knit.

Rep rnds 1 and 2 until there are 64 sts.

FOOT
Work even in St st until foot measures 7"/17.5cm or 2½"/6.5cm less than desired length.

TOE
Rnd 1 *K6, k2tog; rep from * to end—56 sts.

Rnds 2-7 Knit.

Rnd 8 *K5, k2tog; rep from * to end—48 sts.

Rnds 9-13 Knit.

Rnd 14 *K4, k2tog; rep from * to end—40 sts.

Rnds 15-18 Knit.

Rnd 19 *K3, k2tog; rep from * to end—2 sts.

Rnds 20-22 Knit.

Rnd 23 *K2, k2tog; rep from * to end—24 sts.

Rnds 24 and 25 Knit.

Rnd 26 *K1, k2tog; rep from * to end—16 sts.

Rnd 27 Knit.

Rnd 28 *K2tog; rep from * to end—8 sts.

Break yarn leaving an 8"/20.5cm tail. Thread tail through rem sts, pull tightly to close and secure.

FINISHED MEASUREMENTS

6½"/16.5cm from cuff to heel

Approx 9½"/24cm from heel to toe

MATERIALS

2 3½ oz/100g balls (each approx 225yd/206m) Louet Sales **Gems Sportweight** (wool) in #47 terracotta

One set (5) dpns size 3 (3.25mm) OR SIZE TO OBTAIN GAUGE

GAUGE

28 sts and 36 rnds = 4"/10cm over St st using size 3 (3.25mm) needles.

TAKE TIME TO CHECK GAUGE.

Garter Heel Socks

by Susan Lawrence

This sock is worked from the cuff down, with a mini-heel flap, short-row garter-stitch heel and side-decrease wedge toe.

LEG

Cast on 52 sts. Divide sts evenly over 4 needles. Join, taking care not to twist sts. Place marker for end of rnd and sl marker every rnd.

Rnds 1, 3, 5 and 7 Knit.

Rnds 2, 4 and 6 Purl.

Work as foll:

Leg Pattern (Multiple of 13 sts)

Rnd 1 [K1, yo, k3, ssk, p1, k2tog, k3, yo, k1] 4 times.

Rnd 2 Knit.

Rep rnds 1 and 2 until leg measures 6 ½"/16.5cm from beg or desired length to heel.

HEEL

Heel is worked over previous 26 sts. Turn.

Mini-heel flap

Rows 1, 3 and 5 (WS) Sl 1, k24, p1, turn.

Rows 2, 4 and 6 Sl 1, k25, turn.

Row 7 Sl 1, k24, p1, turn.

Short-row heel

Row 1 (RS) Sl 1, k to last st, WT.

Row 2 K to last st, WT.

Row 3 K to 1 st before wrapped st, WT.

Rep row 3 until there are 8 unwrapped sts, end with a WS row.

Next row K to wrapped st, k wrapped st, WT.

Rep last row until first and last heel sts have been wrapped twice, end with a WS row (one st

on RH needle, 25 sts on LH needle). With RH
needle, k12.

GUSSETS

For Needle 1, k13, pick up and k4 along side of
heel flap; for Needles 2 and 3, cont in Leg pat as
est; for Needle 4, pick up and k4 sts along side
of heel flap, k13—60 sts. Place marker for end
of rnd.

Shape gussets

Rnd 1 For Needle 1, k to last 3 sts, k2tog, k1; for
Needles 2 and 3, work in Leg pat as est; for
Needle 4, k1, ssk, k to end.

Rnd 2 Work in pats as est.

Rep rnds 1 and 2 until 52 sts rem.

FOOT

Work even in pats as est until foot measures
7¾"/19.5cm from back of heel or 1¾"/4.5cm less
than desired length.

TOE

Rnd 1 *For Needle 1, k to last 3 sts, k2tog, k1;
for Needle 2, k1, ssk, k to end; rep from * for
needles 3 and 4.

Rnd 2 Knit.

Rep rnds 1 and 2 until 32 sts rem. Rep rnd 1
until 8 sts rem.

Break yarn leaving a 12"/30.5cm tail. Thread tail
through rem sts, draw tightly and secure.

FINISHED MEASUREMENTS
Approx 9½"/24cm from heel to toe

MATERIALS
1 3½ oz/100g ball (approx 466yd/420m) Meilenweit
Fantasy (wool/nylon) in #4760 (A)
1 3½ oz/100g ball (approx 466yd/420m) Meilenweit
Multieffekt (wool/nylon) in #3125 (B)
1 3½ oz/100g ball (approx 466yd/420m) Meilenweit
Meeting (wool/nylon) in #7710 (C)
One set (5) dpns size 2 (2.75mm) OR SIZE TO
OBTAIN GAUGE

GAUGE
30 sts and 40 rnds = 4"/10cm over St st using size 2
(2.75mm) needles.
TAKE TIME TO CHECK GAUGE.

Sockies

by Laura Grutzeck

This "legless" sock is knit from the toe up with

short-row toe and heel. Stitches are picked up around

the foot opening for ribbing. Sockies are the perfect

project for your leftover sock yarns—you can work

stripes randomly in your choice of colors.

Color Patterns

Sockie #1

Work toe with A (start with green)

Work 10 rnds C (start with gray)

Work 24 rnds/rows B (start with gray & white)

Work 12 rnds/rows A

Work 6 rnds/rows C

Complete with B

Work ribbing in B (gray & white)

Sockie #2

Work toe and 7 rnds with B (start with charcoal)

Work 10 rnds C (start with dk gray)

Work 10 rnds A (start at end of orange & white)

Work 21 rnds/rows B

Work 9 rnds/rows C

Complete with A

Work ribbing in B (gray & white)

TOE

Using crochet provisional cast-on (see page 27), cast on 30 sts.

Preparation row Purl.

Row 1 (RS) K to last st, WT.

Row 2 P to last st, WT.

Row 3 K to one st before last wrapped st, WT.

Row 4 P to one st before last wrapped st, WT.

Rep rows 3 and 4 until there are 8 wrapped sts at each end of the needle, ending with a WS row.

Next row K to next wrapped st, WW, WT.

Next row P to next wrapped st, WW, WT.

Rep last 2 rows until all wrapped sts have been worked.

FOOT

Remove waste yarn carefully and divide 60 sts evenly onto 4 needles, picking up an extra st if necessary. Cont Color Pat, work even in St st until foot measures 5"/12.5cm or desired length to ankle.

Next rnd K34, bind off 22 sts for top of sockie (1 st on RH needle), k3—38 sts. Divide evenly over 2 needles and turn.

Sole

Note

Worked back and forth in rows.

Next row (WS) K1, p to last st, k1.

Next row Knit.

Rep last 2 rows until foot measures 7½"/19cm or 2"/5cm less than desired length, ending with a RS row.

Next row K1, p3, pm, p to last 4 sts, pm, p3, k1.

HEEL

K4, beg with row 1 work same as toe over 30 sts between markers, except rep those last 2 rows until there is one wrapped st at each end.

Next row K to next wrapped st, WW, remove marker and k4.

Next row K1, p to next wrapped st, WW, remove marker and p3, k1.

Last row K2tog, *k2tog, pass first st over second st (one st bound off); rep from * to end. Fasten off.

CUFF

With RS facing, starting at last bound-off st, pick up and k19 sts across left side of opening, 22 sts across top, 19 sts across right side and 18 sts across bound-off heel sts—78 sts. Join and work in k1, p1 rib for 4 rnds. Bind off.

FINISHED MEASUREMENTS

10½"/26.5cm circumference

Approx 8½"/21.5cm foot length

MATERIALS

5 1¾/50g balls (each approx 110yd/101m) Naturally NZ

Perendale (wool) #82 burgundy

One set (5) dpns size 5 (3.75mm) OR SIZE TO

OBTAIN GAUGE

Tapestry needle

GAUGE

23 sts and 28 rows = 4"/10cm over St st using size 5

(3.75mm) needles.

TAKE TIME TO CHECK GAUGE.

Renaissance Socks

by Margaret Stove

These socks are worked from the cuff down with

ankle shaping and eyelets at the ankles to hold

twisted cord ties. The heel is turned using an unusual

short-row shaping. The leg pattern continues down

the instep and through the wedge-shaped toe.

Chart 1: Leg

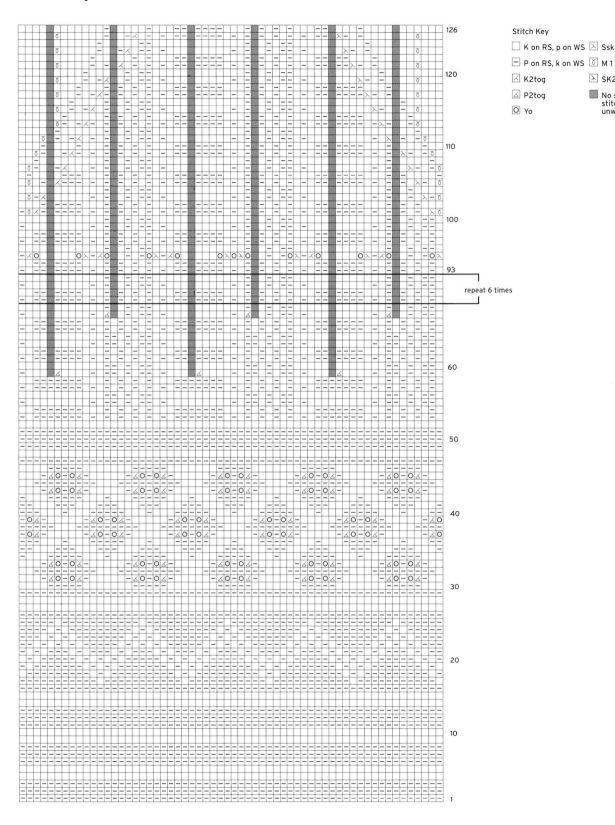

Stitch Key

☐ K on RS, p on WS ◩ Ssk

▭ P on RS, k on WS ⬚ M 1

◪ K2tog ▧ SK2P

◿ P2tog ▨ No stitches or
stitches left
unworked

◯ Yo

repeat 6 times

Chart 2: Toe

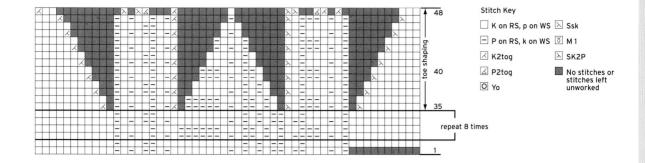

Stitch Key

☐ K on RS, p on WS   ⤬ Ssk

⊟ P on RS, k on WS   🛈 M 1

⤡ K2tog

⤢ P2tog   ⤬ SK2P

⊙ Yo   ■ No stitches or stitches left unworked

LEG

Cast on 60 sts and divide evenly onto 3 needles. Join, taking care not to twist sts. Place marker for end of rnd and sl marker every rnd. Work 68 rnds of Chart 1—54 sts. Rep rnds 69–72 a total of 6 times, then work rnds 93 and 94, eyelet rnd 95, and rnds 96–100.

HEEL

Shape heel seams

Work Rnds 101–126 of Chart 1.

Turn heel

Note Heel turn is worked over 27 sts. Sl first 13 sts of Needle 1 to spare dpn, sl next 27 sts onto Needles 2 and 3 for instep to be worked later, then leave 14 sts on Needle 3 for heel—27 heel sts on spare dpn and Needle 3.

Row 1 (RS) Beg with sts on spare dpn, k3, WT.
Row 2 P7, WT.
Row 3 K to next wrapped st, WW, WT.

Row 4 P to next wrapped st, WW, WT.
Rows 5-20 Rep rows 3 and 4.
Row 21 K to next wrapped st, WW.

FOOT

With 13 sts on Needle 1, beg row 1, sts 14–40 of Chart 2 over Needles 2 and 3, sts 41–54 over Needle 4—54 sts. Work rnd 2 of Chart 2, working WW at wrapped st, then rep rnds 3–6 a total of 8 times or until 2"/5cm less than desired length ending with rnd 6.

TOE

Work rnds 35–48 of Chart 2—16 sts. With Needle 4, k4 from Needle 1. Sl 4 from Needle 2 to Needle 3. Graft toe sts using Kitchener st (see Chapter 2).

FINISHING

Block socks, being careful not to flatten. Make two 30"/75cm twisted cords (see Appendix) and draw through eyelet rnds on socks.

FINISHED MEASUREMENTS

7"/18cm from cuff to heel

Approx 9½"/24cm from heel to toe

MATERIALS

2 3½ oz/100g balls (each approx 225yd/206m) Louet Sales **Gems Sportweight** (wool) in #51 pink panther

One set (5) dpns size 1 (2.25mm) OR SIZE TO OBTAIN GAUGE

GAUGE

28 sts and 44 rows = 4"/10cm over St st using size 1 (2.5mm) needles.

TAKE TIME TO CHECK GAUGE.

Zigzag Socks

by Christine Walter

This sock has a flap heel, with the heel stitch extended through the heel turn, and a star toe.

Pattern Stitch

Zigzag St (multiple of 8 sts)

Rnds 1, 2, 4 and 6 *P1, k6, p1; rep from * to end.

Rnd 3 *P1, yo, k2, ssk, k2, p1; rep from * to end.

Rnd 5 *P1, k1, yo, k2, ssk, k1, p1; rep from * to end.

Rnd 7 *P1, k2, yo, k2, ssk, p1; rep from * to end.

Rnds 8, 9, 10, 12 and 14 *P1, k6, p1; rep from * to end.

Rnd 11 *P1, k2, k2tog, k2, yo, p1; rep from * to end.

Rnd 13 *P1, k1, k2tog, k2, yo, k1, p1; rep from * to end.

Rnd 15 *P1, k2tog, k2, yo, k2, p1; rep from * to end.

Rnd 16 *P1, k6, p1; rep from * to end.

Rep rnds 1–16.

LEG

Cast on 64 sts. Divide sts evenly over 4 needles. Join, taking care not to twist sts. Place marker for end of rnd and sl marker every rnd.

Work in k2, p2 rib for 15 rnds as foll: P1, *k2, p2; rep from *, end last rep p1.

Work rows 1–16 of Zigzag st 3 times, then rows 1–8 once.

HEEL

Heel flap

Worked back and forth over next 32 sts.

Row 1 (RS) *Sl 1, k1; rep from * to end, turn.

Zigzag Stitch

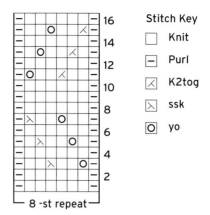

Stitch Key

- ☐ Knit
- ⊟ Purl
- ⊠ K2tog
- ⊠ ssk
- ⊡ yo

8 -st repeat

Row 2 Sl 1, p to end, turn.

Rows 3–30 Rep rows 1 and 2.

Turn heel

Row 31 Sl 1, [k1, sl 1] 8 times, k1, ssk, k1, turn.

Row 32 Sl 1, p5, p2tog, p1, turn.

Row 33 Sl 1, [k1, sl 1] 4 times, ssk, k1, turn.

Row 34 Sl 1, p7, p2tog, p1, turn.

Row 35 Sl 1, k1, [k1, sl 1] 3 times, k1, ssk, k1, turn.

Row 36 Sl 1, p9, p2tog, p1, turn.

Row 37 Sl 1, [k1, sl 1] 5 times, ssk, k1, turn.

Row 38 Sl 1, p11, p2tog, p1, turn.

Row 39 Sl 1, k1, [k1, sl 1] 5 times, k1, ssk, k1, turn.

Row 40 Sl 1, p13, p2tog, p1, turn.

Row 41 Sl 1, [k1, sl 1] 7 times, ssk, k1, turn.

Row 42 Sl 1, p15, p2tog, p1, turn.

Row 43 Sl 1, k1, [k1, sl 1] 7 times, k1, ssk, turn.

Row 44 P17, p2tog, turn—18 sts.

GUSSETS

With RS facing, k9 with spare dpn. With Needle 1, k9 then pick up and k16 sts along side of heel flap; with Needles 2 and 3, cont in pat across next 32 sts, with Needle 4, pick up and k16 sts along side of heel flap, k9 from spare dpn—82 sts. Place marker for end of rnd.

Shape gussets

Rnd 1 For Needle 1, k to last 3 sts, k2tog, k1; for Needles 2 and 3, cont in pat; for Needle 4, k1, ssk, k to end.

Rnd 2 Work even in St st on Needles 1 and 4 and Zigzag st on Needles 2 and 3.

Rep rnds 1 and 2 until 16 sts rem on each needle—64 sts.

FOOT

Work even in pats as est until foot measures 7 ½"/19cm or 2"/5cm from desired length.

TOE

Rnd 1 Knit.

Rnd 2 For Needle 1, *k to last 2 sts, k2tog; rep from * for Needles 2, 3 and 4.

Rnd 3 Knit.

Rep rnds 2 and 3 until there are 40 sts.

Rep rnd 2 until there are 8 sts.

Break yarn, leaving an 8"/20.5cm tail. Thread yarn through rem sts, pull up tightly to close toe and fasten securely.

FINISHED MEASUREMENTS

5½"/14cm from cuff to heel

Approx 10"/25.5cm from heel to toe

MATERIALS

2 1¾ oz/50g balls (each approx 175yd/160m)
Koigu Wool Designs **KPM** (wool) in #1515 jade

One set (5) dpns size 1 (2.25mm) OR SIZE TO
OBTAIN GAUGE

GAUGE

30 sts and 44 rnds = 4"/10cm over St st using size 1
(2.5mm) needles.

TAKE TIME TO CHECK GAUGE.

Leaf Lace Socks

by Susan Lawrence

This sock is worked from the cuff down,

beginning with a picot hem. The heel flap is

worked with eye-of-partridge stitch and

the sock is finished with a grafted toe.

Chart 1

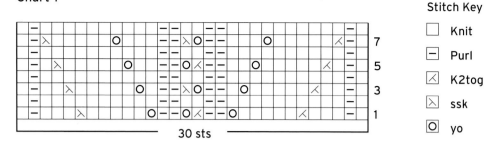

30 sts

Chart 2

5-st repeat

Stitch Key

☐	Knit
−	Purl
⊿	K2tog
⋊	ssk
◎	yo

Pattern Stitches

Leaf Lace (worked over 30 sts)

Rnd 1 K1, p1, k3, k2tog, k5, yo, p2, k2tog, yo, p2, yo, k5, ssk, k3, p1, k1.

Rnds 2, 4 and 6 K1, p1, k10, p2, k2, p2, k10, p1, k1.

Rnd 3 K1, p1, k2, k2tog, k5, yo, k1, p2, yo, ssk, p2, k1, yo, k5, ssk, k2, p1, k1.

Rnd 5 K1, p1, k1, k2tog, k5, yo, k2, p2, k2tog, yo, p2, k2, yo, k5, ssk, k1, p1, k1.

Rnd 7 K1, p1, k2tog, k5, yo, k3, p2, yo, ssk, p2, k3, yo, k5, ssk, p1, k1.

Rnd 8 Rep rnd 2.

Rep rnds 1–8.

Ladder Lace (multiple of 5 sts)

Rnd 1 [K2tog, yo, k1, yo, ssk] 6 times.

Rnd 2 Knit.

Rep rnds 1 and 2.

LEG

Loosely cast on 60 sts. Divide sts evenly over 4 needles. Join, taking care not to twist sts. Place marker for end of rnd and sl marker every rnd.

Rnds 1–5 Knit.

Rnd 6 *Yo, k2tog; rep from * to end.

Rnds 7–12 Knit.

Fold hem to inside of sock along eyelet rnd (rnd 6). Place loop of first cast-on st onto LH needle and knit together with st on needle. Rep until all cast-on sts have been worked.

K 1 rnd, redistributing sts as foll: 17 sts on Needle 1, 13 sts on Needle 2, 15 sts each on Needles 3 and 4.

Work 8 rnds of Leaf Lace pat (Chart 1) seven times over Needles 1 and 2 and Ladder Lace pat (Chart 2) over Needles 3 and 4.

HEEL

Heel flap

Worked over last 30 sts.

Rows 1 and 3 (WS) Sl 1, p29, turn.

Row 2 *Sl 1, k1; rep from * to end, turn.

Row 4 Sl 1, *sl 1, k1; rep from *, end k1, turn.

Rep rows 1–4 six times more, then rep row 1 once—29 rows total.

Turn heel

Row 1 Sl 1, k16, ssk, k1, turn.

Row 2 Sl 1, p5, p2tog, p1, turn.

Row 3 Sl 1, k to one st before gap, ssk, k1, turn.

Row 4 Sl 1, p to one st before gap, p2tog, p1, turn.

Rep rows 3 and 4 until all sts have been worked —18 sts.

GUSSETS

With spare dpn, k9. With Needle 1, k9 then pick up and k15 sts along side of heel flap; with Needle 2, cont in pat across 17 instep sts; with Needle 3, cont in pat across rem 13 instep sts; with Needle 4, pick up and k15 sts along side of heel flap, k9 from spare dpn—78 sts. Place marker for end of rnd.

Shape gussets

Rnd 1 For Needle 1, k to last 3 sts, k2tog, k1, cont in Leaf Lace pat across Needles 2 and 3, for Needle 4, k1, ssk, k to end.

Rnd 2 Work even in St st on Needles 1 and 4 and Leaf Lace pat on Needles 2 and 3.

Rep rnds 1 and 2 until 60 sts rem.

FOOT

Work even in pats as est until foot measures approx 8¼"/21cm or 1¾"/4.5cm from desired length, end with row 8 of pat.

TOE

Rnd 1 Knit.

Rnd 2 *For Needle 1, k to last 3 sts, k2tog, k1, for Needle 2, k1, ssk, k to end; rep from * for Needles 3 and 4.

Rep rnds 1 and 2 until there are 32 sts.

Rep rnd 2 until there are 12 sts.

With Needle 4, k3 from Needle 1. Sl sts from Needle 2 onto Needle 3.

Graft toe sts using Kitchener st (see Chapter 2).

Diamond Lace Socks

by Joan McGowan-Michael

This sock is worked from the toe up with

a decrease/increase toe and heel.

FINISHED MEASUREMENTS

5¼"/13.5cm from cuff to heel

Approx 9"/23cm from heel to toe

MATERIALS

1 3½ oz/100g ball (approx 459yd/420m) Zitron/Skacel Collection, Inc. **Trekking XXL** (wool/nylon) in #78 purples.

One set (5) dpns size 3 (3.25mm) OR SIZE TO OBTAIN GAUGE

GAUGE

29 sts and 36 rnds = 4"/10cm over St st using size 3 (3.25mm) needles.

TAKE TIME TO CHECK GAUGE.

Pattern stitch

Diamond Lace Pat (multiple of 7 sts)

Rnd 1 and all odd-numbered rnds Knit.

Rnd 2 *K2, k2tog, yo, k3; rep from *.

Rnd 4 *K1, k2tog, yo, k1, yo, ssk, k1; repfrom *.

Rnd 6 *K2tog, yo, k3, yo, ssk; rep from *.

Rnd 8 *K2tog, yo, k2, k2tog, yo, k1; rep from *.

Rnd 10 K2, yo, k3tog, yo, k2; rep from *.

Rep rnds 1–10.

TOE

Using provisional crochet cast-on (see page 27), cast on 28 sts.

Row 1 (WS) Purl.

Row 2 K1, ssk, k to last 3 sts, k2tog, k1.

Rep rows 1 and 2 until 8 sts rem.

Next row Purl.

Next row Pick up and k1 from end of previous RS row on first half of toe, k to end, pick up and k1 from first half of toe as before.

Rep last 2 rows until there are 28 sts.

FOOT

Carefully remove waste yarn and slip 28 sts evenly over 2 dpns, divide rem 28 sts over 2 dpns—56 sts. K28, pm for end of rnd. For Needles 1 and 2, work in Diamond Lace pat for instep and for Needles 3 and 4, work in St st for sole until foot measures 7"/18cm or 2"/5cm less

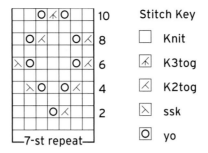

			O	⋏	O		10
	O	⋉			O	⋉	8
⋋	O				O	⋉	6
	⋋	O		O	⋉		4
		O	⋉				2

└─7-st repeat─┘

Stitch Key

☐ Knit

⋏ K3tog

⋉ K2tog

⋋ ssk

O yo

than desired length. Turn.

HEEL

Work back and forth as for toe starting with Row 1 over 28 sts of sole.

LEG

Cont in Diamond Lace pat over all 56 sts until

leg measures 3"/7.5cm from top of heel or 2½"/6.5cm less than desired length. Work in k4, p4 rib for 2½"/6.5cm. Bind off loosely in rib.

Graft toe sts using Kitchener st (see Chapter 2). Weave in ends.

FINISHED MEASUREMENTS

7"/17.5cm from cuff to heel

Approx 8"/20.5cm from heel to toe

MATERIALS

2 3½ oz/100g skeins (each approx 459yd/420m) of
Zitron/Skacel Collection, Inc. **Trekking XXL** (wool/nylon)
in #133 cotton candy

Two circular needles, size 6 (4mm) 24"/60cm long OR

SIZE TO OBTAIN GAUGE

Size G/6 (4mm) crochet hook for cast-on

Tapestry needle

Flow Motion Socks

by Cat Bordhi

These socks are knit from the toe up using

two circular needles. The unique figure-eight cast-on

is explained below.

GAUGE

24 sts and 34 rnds = 4"/10cm over St st using 2 strands
held tog and size 6 (4mm) needles.

TAKE TIME TO CHECK GAUGE.

Notes

To knit in the round with two circular needles, divide stitches on two needles as directed, join (being sure cast-on is not twisted), and use each needle to knit its own stitches. When first needle is finished, its stitches are slid to the middle (cable) section of the needle, and the circle of needles rotates clockwise. The yarn passes counterclockwise from first needle to the second needle, which then knits its own stitches. The second needle rests with its stitches in the middle and passes the yarn to first needle—one needle works while the other rests.

The figure-eight cast-on places stitches on two parallel needles, alternately on the top needle, then the bottom needle, top, then bottom, etc. It is a provisional cast-on suitable for toe-up socks. Hold two circular needles in one hand so that the top needles are parallel. Bring the yarn between the needles and leaving a tail of about 5", begin snugly wrapping the yarn around the two tips in a figure-eight, so that the two tips fill the two holes in the "8." Wrap until there are several more stitches on each needle than required. On the first round only, either the first or the second needle will have stitches mounted with the leading leg in back, which means that this needle's stitches will have to be knit through the back. Pull the bottom needle so that it hangs down with its stitches resting on its cable. Use both ends of the top needle to knit the required number of stitches, then push the extras off the needle, allowing them to fall from the other needle as well. Pull the top needle so its just-knitted stitches rest on its cable and rotate it clockwise, with the right side still facing you and the ends of this needle hanging down. Use both ends of the other needle (which is now on top) to knit its stitches (which ought to be identical to the number of stitches just knit on the first needle).

TOE

Using figure-eight cast-on, cast on 20 sts (10 on each needle). K 2 rnds.

Toe increases

Rnd 1 For Needle 1, *k2, M1R, k to last 2 sts, M1L, k2; rep from * for 2nd needle.

Rnd 2 Knit.

Rep rnds 1 and 2 until there are 44 sts.

FOOT

Cont in St st until foot measures 5¼"/14cm, or 3¾"/9.5cm less than desired length.

Instep

Work instep chart or as foll:

Rnds 1 and 2 K10, k2 tbl, k32.

Rnd 3 K10, k1 tbl, yo, k1 tbl, k32.

Rnd 4 K9, k2 tbl, k1, k2 tbl, k31.

Rnd 5 K9, k2 tbl, yo, k1 tbl, yo, k2 tbl, k31.

Rnd 6 K9, k2 tbl, k1, k1 tbl, k1, k2 tbl, k31.

Rnd 7 K9, k2 tbl, yo, k3 tbl, yo, k2 tbl, k31.

Rnd 8 K9, k2 tbl, k1, k3 tbl, k1, k2 tbl, k31.

Rnd 9 K9, k4 tbl, yo, k1 tbl, yo, k4 tbl, k31.

Rnd 10 K9, k4 tbl, k1, k1 tbl, k1, k4 tbl, k31.

Rnd 11 K8, k5 tbl, yo, k3 tbl, yo, k5 tbl, k30.

Rnd 12 K7, k6 tbl, k1, k3 tbl, k1, k6 tbl, k29.

Rnd 13 K7, k6 tbl, yo, k5 tbl, yo, k6 tbl, k29.

Rnd 14 K7, k6 tbl, k1, k5 tbl, k1, k6 tbl, k29.

Rnd 15 K7, k6 tbl, yo, k7 tbl, yo, k6 tbl, k29.

Rnd 16 K7, k6 tbl, k1, k7 tbl, k1, k6 tbl, k29.

Rnd 17 K7, k10 tbl, yo, k1 tbl, yo, k10 tbl, k29.

Rnd 18 K7, k10 tbl, k1, k1 tbl, k1, k10 tbl, k29.

Rnd 19 K7, k10 tbl, yo, k3 tbl, yo, k10 tbl, k29.

Rnd 20 K7, k10 tbl, k1, k3 tbl, k1, k10 tbl, k29.

Rnd 21 K7, k6 tbl, yo, k4 tbl, yo, k5 tbl, yo, k4 tbl, yo, k6 tbl, k29.

Rnd 22 K7, k6 tbl, k1, k4 tbl, k1, k2 tbl, p1, k2 tbl, k1, k4 tbl, k1, k6 tbl, k29.

Rnd 23 K7, k6 tbl, yo, k1 tbl, yo, k4 tbl, k2tog, p1, k1, p1, ssk, k4 tbl, yo, k1 tbl, yo, k6 tbl, k29.

Rnd 24 K7, k6 tbl, k1, k1 tbl, k1, k4 tbl, k2, p1, k2, k4 tbl, k1, k1 tbl, k1, k6 tbl, k29.

Rnd 25 K7, k6 tbl, yo, k3 tbl, yo, k3 tbl, k2tog, p1, k1, p1, ssk, k3 tbl, yo, k3 tbl, yo, k6 tbl, k29.

Rnd 26 K7, k6 tbl, k1, k3 tbl, k1, k3 tbl, k2, p1, k2, k3 tbl, k1, k3 tbl, k1, k6 tbl, k7.

(Do not knit across sole needle.)

HEEL

Turn Heel

Note You should have 22 sts on the sole needle and 47 sts on the instep needle. Work short rows on sole needle only.

Row 1 (RS) K1, sl 1, k18, WT.

Row 2 Sl 1, p17, WT.

Row 3 Sl 1, k16, WT.

Row 4 Sl 1, p15, WT.

Row 5 Sl 1, k14, WT.

Row 6 Sl 1, p13, WT.

Row 7 Sl 1, k12, WT.

Row 8 Sl 1, p11, WT.

Row 9 Sl 1, k10, WT.

Row 10 Sl 1, p9, WT.

Row 11 Sl 1, k9, [WW] 5 times.

Slip next st. Move adjacent 12 sts from instep needle to sole needle. Move 12 sts from other end of instep needle to other end of sole needle—23 sts on instep needle, 46 sts on sole needle. Arrange sts on sole needle so you can resume knitting where the yarn is waiting, checking to be sure you are on a knit side.

Next row Ssk, turn. Sl 1, p15, [WW] 5 times, p2tog, turn.

Heel Flap

Row 1 (RS) *Sl 1, k1; rep from * 9 times more, sl 1, ssk, turn.

Row 2 Sl 1, p20, p2tog, turn.

Rep rows 1 and 2 until 22 sts rem on this needle, ending with a WS row, turn.

Final row Sl 1, k10, M1, k11.

LEG

Note Resume working in rnds, beg on instep needle.

Work Leg Chart or as foll:

Rnd 1 With instep needle, pick up and k1 tbl in intersection between needles, k1 tbl, yo, k5 tbl, yo, k2 tbl, k2tog, p1, k1, p1, ssk, k2 tbl, yo, k5 tbl, yo, k1 tbl, pick up and k1 in intersection; with sole needle, k2tog, p1, k1, p1, ssk, k2 tbl, yo, k5 tbl, yo, k2 tbl, k2tog, p1, k1, p1, ssk— 48 sts.

Instep Chart

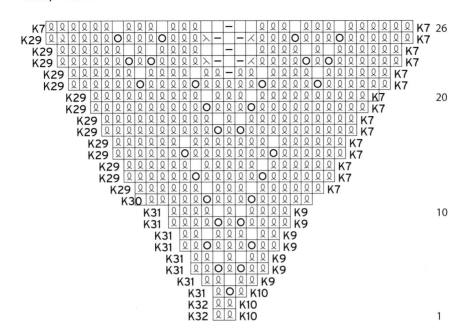

Stich Key

☐	K on RS, p on WS
—	P on RS, k on WS
╱	K2tog
╲	ssk
○	Yo
ℚ	K1 tbl
☐	No Stitch

Leg Chart

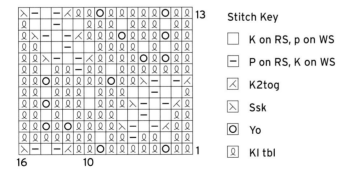

Stitch Key

☐	K on RS, p on WS
—	P on RS, K on WS
╱	K2tog
╲	Ssk
○	Yo
ℚ	KI tbl

Rnd 2 [K2 tbl, k1, k2 tbl, p1, k2 tbl, k1, k7 tbl] 3 times.

Rnd 3 [K2 tbl, k2tog, p1, k1, p1, ssk, k4 tbl, yo, k1 tbl, yo, k2 tbl] 3 times.

Rnd 4 [K2 tbl, k2, p1, k2, k4 tbl, k1, k1 tbl, k1, k2 tbl] 3 times.

Rnd 5 [K1 tbl, k2tog, p1, k1, p1, ssk, k3 tbl, yo, k3 tbl, yo, k2 tbl] 3 times.

Rnd 6 [K1 tbl, k2, p1, k2, k3 tbl, k1, k3 tbl, k1, k2 tbl] 3 times.

Rnd 7 [K2tog, p1, k1, p1, ssk, k2 tbl, yo, k5 tbl, yo, k2 tbl] 3 times.

Rnd 8 [K7 tbl, k1, k2 tbl, p1, k2 tbl, k1, k2 tbl] 3 times.

Rnd 9 [K2 tbl, yo, k1 tbl, yo, k4 tbl, k2tog, p1, k1, p1, ssk, k2 tbl] 3 times.

Rnd 10 [K2 tbl, k1, k1 tbl, k1, k4 tbl, k2, p1, k2, k2 tbl; rep from * 3 times.

Rnd 11 [K2 tbl, yo, k3 tbl, yo, k3 tbl, k2tog, p1, k1, p1, ssk, k1 tbl] 3 times.

Rnd 12 [K2 tbl, k1, k3 tbl, k1, k3 tbl, k2, p1, k2, k1 tbl] 3 times.

Rnd 13 [K2 tbl, yo, k5 tbl, yo, k2 tbl, k2tog, p1, k1, p1, ssk] 3 times.

Rep rnds 2–13 three times more.

Seed Stitch Picot cuff

Rnds 1, 3 and 5 *K1, p1; rep from * to end.

Rnds 2 and 4 *P1, k1; rep from * to end.

Rnd 6 *Ssk, yo; rep from * to end.

Rnds 7-11 Knit.

Bind off loosely, fold to inside at rnd 6, and sew in place. Weave in all ends.

FINISHED MEASUREMENTS

3½"/9cm from cuff to heel

Approx 9½"/24cm from heel to toe

MATERIALS

1 1¾ oz/50g ball (approx 222yd/203m) Brown Sheep Company **Cotton Fine** (cotton/wool) each in #CF810 cherry moon (MC), #CF520 caribbean sea (A), #CF310 wild orange (B) and #CF840 lime light (C).

Two 24"/60cm circular needles sizes 0 and 1 (2 and 2.25mm) OR SIZE TO OBTAIN GAUGE

GAUGE

36 sts and 46 rnds = 4"/10cm over St st using size 0 (2mm) needles.

TAKE TIME TO CHECK GAUGE.

Note

To use double-pointed needles instead of two circulars, divide the stitches of each circular needle onto two dpns.

Ornate Socks

by Patti Pierce Stone

This anklet is knit from the cuff down on two circular needles with a two-color purl slip-stitch heel and a round toe.

For knitters with an inordinate fear of double-pointed needles, knitting a sock on two circular needles is a great solution. With half the stitches on each needle there are only two places where you would swap needles, and even then there are no needles to drop since you are picking up the end of a circular needle.

MB (make bobble) K into front, back and front of next st, turn. P3, turn, k3, turn, p3, turn, SK2P.

CUFF

2-Color cast-on With MC and A held tog, loosely tie a slipknot approx 6"/15cm from end. Place on larger needle and with A over thumb and MC over index finger, cast on 72 sts (excluding slipknot) using long tail cast-on. Divide sts evenly over 2 circular needles. Join, taking care not to twist sts. Place marker for end of rnd and sl marker every rnd.

Rnd 1 With A, *sl 1, k1; rep from * to end.

Rnd 2 With MC, *k1, p1; rep from * to end.

Rep rnds 1 and 2 eight times more.

LEG

Bobble band (multiple of 3 sts)

Rnds 1 and 2 With MC, knit.

Rnd 3 With MC, *k1, sl 1; rep from * to end.

Rnd 4 With A, *loosely sl 1, k1; rep from * to end.

Rnd 5 *Pass 2nd st on LH needle over first st and off needle. With MC, kfb next st; rep from * to end.

Rnd 6 With MC, knit.

Rnd 7 With MC, k1, sl 1, *k2, sl 1; rep from *, end k1.

Rnd 8 With B, sl 1, k1, *sl 2, k1; rep from *, end sl 1.

Rnd 9 With B, sl 1, MB, *sl 2, MB; rep from *, end sl 1.

Rnds 10 and 11 With MC, knit.

Rnd 12 With MC, *k1, sl 1; rep from * to end.

Rnd 13 With A, *loosely sl 1, k1; rep from * to end.

Rnd 14 Rep rnd 5

Rnd 15 With MC, knit.

Dots (multiple of 2 sts)

Rnd 1 With C, *sl 1, k1; rep from * to end.

Rnd 2 With MC, *k1, p1; rep from * to end.

Rnd 3 With MC, knit.

Rnd 4 With C, *k1, sl 1; rep from * to end.

Rnd 5 With MC, *p1, k1; rep from * to end.

Rnd 6 With MC, knit.

Rnds 7-18 Rep rnds 1-6 twice or to ½"/1.5cm less than desired length to top of heel.

Rnd 19 With MC, *k1, sl 1; rep from * to end.

Rnd 20 With A, *loosely sl 1, k1; rep from * to end.

Rnd 21 *Pass 2nd st on LH needle over first st and off needle. With MC, kfb next st; rep from * to end. Change to smaller needles.

Rnds 22-24 With MC, knit.

HEEL

With MC, k37 (instep sts). Heel is worked over next 35 sts.

Row 1 (RS) With A, sl 1 wyib, *p1, sl 1 wyif; rep from *, end sl 1 wyib.

Row 2 (RS) Slide sts back to other end of needle. With MC, k2, *p1, k1; rep from *, end k1, turn.

Row 3 (WS) With A, sl 1 wyif, *k1, sl 1 wyib; rep from *, end sl 1 wyif.

Row 4 (WS) Slide sts back to other end of needle. With MC, p2, *k1, p1; rep from *, end p1, turn. Rep rows 1–4 nine times more.

Turn heel

With RS facing, join B and k35.

Row 1 P19, p2tog, p1, turn.

Row 2 Sl 1, k4, ssk, k1, turn.

Row 3 Sl 1, p to 1 st before gap, p2tog, p1, turn.

Row 4 Sl 1, k to 1 st before gap, ssk, k1, turn. Rep rows 3 and 4 until all heel sts have been worked, omitting p1 and k1 at end of last 2 rows—19 sts. Break off B.

GUSSETS

With RS facing and Needle 1, join MC and k across 37 instep sts. With Needle 2, pick up and k1 in corner between instep and heel, pick up and k18 sts tbl along side of heel flap, k19 heel sts, pick up and k18 sts tbl along side of heel flap, pick up and k1 in corner—94 sts. Pm for end of rnd.

Shape gussets

Rnd 1 For Needle 1, knit. For Needle 2, k1, ssk, k to last 3 sts, k2tog, k1.

Rnd 2 Knit.

Rep rnds 1 and 2 until 70 sts rem.

FOOT

Work even in St st until foot measures 7½"/19cm from back of heel or 2"/5cm less than desired length. Break off MC.

Toe

Slip first 4 and last 5 sts of Needle 1 onto Needle 2 and move marker—(Needle 1: 28 sts, Needle 2: 42 sts).

Rnd 1 Knit.

Rnd 2 *K12, k2tog; rep from * to end—65 sts.

Rnds 3 and 4 Knit.

Rnd 5 *K11, k2tog; rep from * to end—60 sts.

Rnds 6 and 7 Knit.

Rnd 8 *K10, k2tog; rep from * to end—55 sts.

Rnds 9 and 10 Knit.

Rnd 11 *K9, k2tog; rep from * to end—50 sts.

Rnds 12, 14 and 16 Knit.

Rnd 13 *K8, k2tog; rep from * to end—45 sts.

Rnd 15 *K7, k2tog; rep from * to end—40 sts.

Rnd 17 *K6, k2tog; rep from * to end—35 sts.

Rnd 18 *K5, k2tog; rep from * to end—30 sts.

Rnd 19 *K4, k2tog; rep from * to end—25 sts.

Rnd 20 *K3, k2tog; rep from * to end—20 sts.

Rnd 21 *K2, k2tog; rep from * to end—15 sts.

Rnd 22 *K1, k2tog; rep from * to end—10 sts.

Break yarn leaving a 6"/15cm tail. Thread through rem 10 sts twice, draw tightly and secure. Release slipknot at cast-on and weave in ends.

FINISHED MEASUREMENTS

7"/18cm from cuff to heel

Approx 9"/24cm from heel to toe

MATERIALS

1 3½ oz/100g hank (approx 225yd/206m) Louet Sales Gems **Sportweight** each in #21 cloud grey (A) and #57 french blue (B)

One set (5) dpns sizes 1 and 2 (2.25 and 2.75mm)

OR SIZE TO OBTAIN GAUGE

GAUGE

36 sts and 36 rows = 4"/10cm over Chart 3 in St st using larger needles.

TAKE TIME TO CHECK GAUGE.

Nordic Star Socks

by Jan Malone

This sock uses traditional Fair Isle motifs and is worked from the cuff down with unusual gusset increases and a short-row heel.

LEG

With larger needles, cast on 72 sts with B. Divide sts evenly over 4 needles. Join, taking care not to twist sts. Place marker for end of rnd and sl marker every rnd. Work in k2, p2 rib for 8 rnds. Work 29 rnds of Chart 1, 14 rnds of Chart 2 beg with st 1 and end with st 12, and 9 rnds of Chart 3.

Gussets

Work 22 rnds of Chart 4 as foll: On Needles 1 and 2, beg with M1 (gusset st), work sts 1–36, M1 (gusset st), and on Needles 3 and 4, work sts 1–36 of Chart 4 ending with st 18 on last rnd (center of heel).

Heel shaping

Working with 36 sts on Needles 3 and 4 only, change to smaller needles and work Chart 5 as foll:

Row 1 (RS) [K1 B, k1 A] twice, k1 B. WT with color of next st.

Row 2 [P1 B, p1 A] 5 times. WT with color of next st.

Row 3 [K1 B, k1 A] 5 times, k1 B. WT with color of next st.

Chart 1

29

20

10

1

36-st repeat

Chart 2

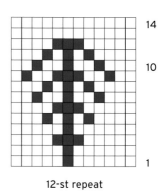

14

10

1

12-st repeat

Chart 3

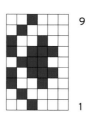

9

1

6-st repeat

Chart 4

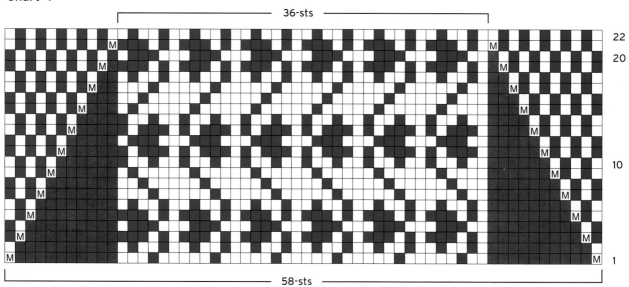

36-sts

22

20

10

1

58-sts

Cont in this manner, working one more st each row and wrapping the next st until all sts on Needles 3 and 4 have been worked.

Gusset decreases

Change to larger needles and cont back and forth on Needles 3 and 4 in pats as est, working gusset sts into sole as foll:

Row 1 Sl 1, pat to last st on Needle 4, ssk (working last st on Needle 4 tog with first st on Needle 1), turn.

Row 2 Sl 1, pat to last st on Needle 3, p2tog (working last st on Needle 3 tog with first st on Needle 2), turn.

Rep rows 1 and 2 until all gusset sts have been worked—72 sts.

FOOT

Cont even in patterns until foot measures 6¾"/17cm or 2¼"/5.5cm from desired length.

TOE

Rnd 1 (dec) *Cont in pat, on Needle 1, ssk, work to last 2 sts of Needle 2, k2tog; rep from * for needles 3 and 4.

Rnd 2 Work even in pats.

Rep rnds 1 and 2 until 12 sts rem. Graft toe sts using Kitchener st (see Chapter 2).

Color Key
☐ A
■ B

Stitch Key
☐ Knit
■ No Stitch
Ⓜ Make 1

Chart 5

24
20
10
1

FINISHED MEASUREMENTS

3½"/9cm from cuff to heel

Approx 4¾"/12cm from heel to toe

MATERIALS

1 1¾ oz/50g ball (approx 191yd/175m) Dale of Norway **Baby Ull** (wool) each in #3718 coral (A) and #2317 gold (B)

One set (5) dpns sizes 0 and 1 (2mm and 2.25mm) OR SIZE TO OBTAIN GAUGE

GAUGE

8 ½ sts and 9 rnds = 1"/2.5cm over heel chart using size 1 (2mm) needles.

TAKE TIME TO CHECK GAUGE.

Toddler Socks

by Risë Burgie

These socks begin with a two-color cast-on and continue with a number of simple two-color Fair Isle patterns throughout. They have a two-color heel flap and wedge toe.

Reverse Long-Tail Cast-On This cast-on uses a bit more yarn on the tail end than the traditional long-tail cast-on since loops are created from the yarn tail. Steps 1 and 2 are the same as long-tail cast-on (see page 49).

Step 1: Bring the yarn tail end around the left thumb from front to back; then wrap the yarn from the ball over the left index finger. Hold the ends firmly in your palm.

Step 2: Insert the right needle upward from the back of the hand in the left index finger loop. With the needle tip, draw the yarn from the yarn tail through the loop to form a stitch.

Step 3: Remove your thumb from the loop and tighten the loop on the needle. It should be firm, but not tight, and should slide easily along the needle. Repeat Steps 1 through 3 for each stitch to be cast on.

CUFF

Using 2 smaller dpns held tog, cast on 48 sts as foll: Using long-tail cast-on (see page 25), cast on 1 B, *using reverse long-tail cast-on, cast on 2 A, long-tail cast-on 2 B—always bringing the 2 ends of the new color outside the old color; rep

Chart 1

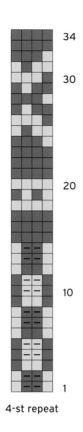

34

30

20

10

1

4-st repeat

Chart 2

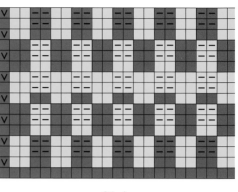

24 sts

Chart 3

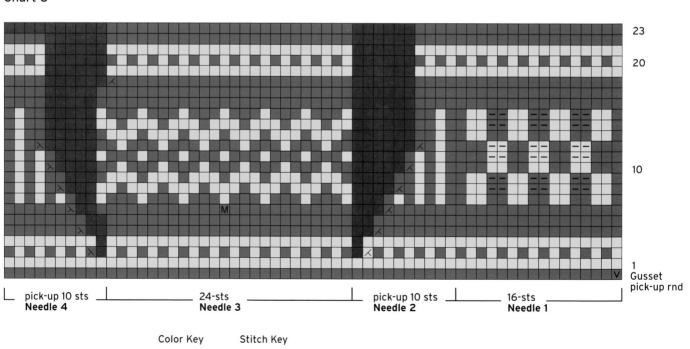

23

20

10

1
Gusset
pick-up rnd

| pick-up 10 sts | 24-sts | pick-up 10 sts | 16-sts |
| Needle 4 | Needle 3 | Needle 2 | Needle 1 |

Color Key
- ☐ A
- ■ B

Stitch Key
- ☐ Knit
- ⊟ Purl
- ■ No Stitch
- M Make 1
- ⬚ K2tog
- ⬚ ssk
- �V Sl 1

Chart 4

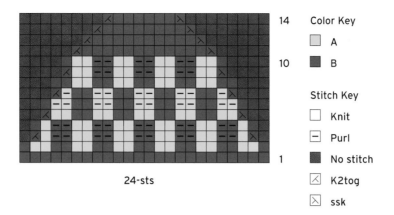

14

10

1

24-sts

Color Key

☐ A

■ B

Stitch Key

☐ Knit

⊟ Purl

■ No stitch

◩ K2tog

◪ ssk

from *, end last rep long-tail cast-on 1 B. Remove extra needle and divide sts evenly over 4 dpns. Join, taking care not to twist sts. Place marker for end of rnd and sl marker every rnd. With smaller dpns, work rnds 1–14 of Chart 1.

LEG

Change to larger dpns and work rnds 15–34 of Chart 1.

HEEL

Change to smaller dpns and work rows 1–16 of Chart 2 over 24 sts on Needles 1 and 2.

Turn heel

Row 1 (RS) With A, sl 1, k14, ssk, k1, turn.
Row 2 Sl 1, p7, p2tog, p1, turn.
Row 3 Sl 1, k to 1 st before gap, ssk, k1, turn.
Row 4 Sl 1, p to 1 st before gap, p2tog, p1, turn.
Rep rows 3 and 4 until all sts have been worked—16 sts. Change to larger dpns.

GUSSETS AND FOOT

Foll pick-up rnd of Chart 3, with Needle 1 and A, sl 1, k15 heel sts; with Needle 2, pick up and k10 sts along side of heel flap; with Needle 3, k24 instep sts; with Needle 4, pick up and k10 sts along side of heel flap—60 sts. Pm for end of rnd.

Work rnds 1–23 of Chart 3, dec and inc as noted and ending with Needle 3, 4 sts from end of rnd. Slip those last 4 sts onto Needle 1. Pm for new end of rnd and redistribute sts evenly over 4 dpns.

TOE

Work 14 rows of Chart 4 over Needles 1 and 2, and rep over Needles 3 and 4. When chart is complete, graft toe sts using Kitchener st (see Chapter 2). For second sock, substitute B for A throughout.

FINISHED MEASUREMENTS

6½"/16.5cm from cuff to heel

Approx 9"/23cm from heel to toe

MATERIALS

2 1¾ oz/50g skeins (approx 175yd/160m) Koigu Wool Designs **KPM** (wool) in #2166 purple

Note

Larger sizes will require an additional skein of yarn.

Two circular needles size 1 (2.25mm) OR SIZE TO OBTAIN GAUGE

GAUGE

32 sts and 44 rnds = 4"/10cm over St st using size 1 (2.25mm) needles.

TAKE TIME TO CHECK GAUGE.

STITCH GLOSSARY

2-st RC Sl 1 st to cn and hold to back, k1 tbl, k1 tbl from cn.

2-st LC Sl 1 st to cn and hold to front, k1 tbl, k1 tbl from cn.

2-st RPC Sl 1 st to cn and hold to back, k1 tbl, p1 from cn.

2-st LPC Sl 1 st to cn and hold to front, p1, k1 tbl from cn.

8-st RPC Sl 4 sts to cn and hold to back, [k1 tbl, p2, k1 tbl], [k1 tbl, p2, k1 tbl] from cn.

CE (chain edge) Sl 1 wyif, return yarn to back of work.

Bavarian Socks

by Candace Eisner Strick

This sock is knit from the cuff down with garter-edged heel flap and wedge toe. Twist-stitch cables are continued from the leg over the instep to the tip of the toe.

CUFF

Cast on 72 sts. Divide sts evenly over 2 needles. Join, taking care not to twist sts. Place marker for end of rnd and sl marker every rnd. Work rnd 1 of Chart eight times for ribbing.

LEG

Work 11 rnds of chart five times, then rnds 1–3.

HEEL

Heel Flap

Worked back and forth over first 36 sts.

Row 1 K3, M1, *sl 1, k1; rep from * to last 5 sts, sl 1, k4—37 sts.

Row 2 CE, k3, p to last 4 sts, k4.

Row 3 CE, k3, *sl 1, k1; rep from * to last 5 sts, sl 1, k4.

Row 4 CE, k3, p to last 4 sts, k4.

Rep rows 3 and 4 until there are 32 rows.

Turn heel

Row 1 K2tog, k19, skp, k1, turn.

Row 2 Sl 1, p5, p2tog, p1, turn.

Row 3 Sl 1, k to 1 st before gap, skp, k1, turn.

Row 4 Sl 1, p to 1 st before gap, p2tog, p1, turn.

Twist-stitch Cable Pattern

36-st repeat

10

1

Stitch Key

−	Purl
Ω	K tbl
	2-st RC
	2-st LC
	2-st LPC
	2-st RPC
	8-st LPC
	8-st RPC

Rep rows 3 and 4 until all heel sts have been worked—20 sts.

GUSSETS

K10, pick up and k17 along side of heel, cont in pat across 36 instep sts (rnd 4 of chart), pick up and k17 along side of heel, k10—90 sts. Pm for end of rnd (center of Needle 1).

Shape gussets

Rnd 1 For Needle 1, k to last 3 sts, k2tog, k1; for Needle 2, cont in pat as est; for Needle 1, k1, skp, k to end of rnd.

Rnd 2 For Needle 1, knit; for Needle 2, work in pat as est.

Rep rnds 1 and 2 until there are 36 sts on Needle 1.

FOOT

Work even in pats as est until foot measures 6½"/16.5cm or 2½"/6.5cm less than desired length.

TOE

Note From this point on, the center 22 sts only of the instep (Needle 2) are worked in pattern. All other sts are worked in St st.

Rnd 1 For Needle 1, k to last 3 sts, k2tog, k1; for Needle 2, k1, ssk, k to center 22 sts and work in pat as est, k to last 3 sts, k2tog, k1; for Needle 1, k1, ssk, k to end of rnd.

Rnd 2 For Needle 1, knit; for Needle 2, work in pat as est.

Rep rnds 1 and 2 until there are 36 sts, then rep rnd 1 only until 8 sts rem. Graft toe sts using Kitchener st (see Chapter 2).

FINISHED MEASUREMENTS

7"/18cm from cuff to heel

Approx 9¼"/23.5cm from heel to toe

MATERIALS

2 1¾ oz/50g skeins (approx 222yd/203m) Brown Sheep
Company **Cotton Fine** (cotton/wool) in #CF-365 peridot (A)

1 skein #CF-210 tea rose (B)

Two circular needles size 1 (2.25mm) OR SIZE TO
OBTAIN GAUGE

Latvian Socks

by Lizbeth Upitis

This sock is knit from the cuff down with scalloped

edge, heel flap and wedge toe.

GAUGE

34 sts and 46 rnds = 4"/10cm over St st using size 1
(2.25mm) needles.

TAKE TIME TO CHECK GAUGE.

Chart 1

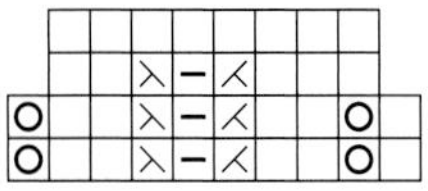

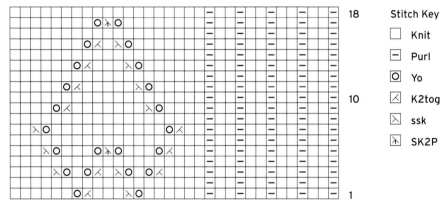

10-st rep

4

1

Stitch Key

☐ Knit

— Purl

◯ Yo

◿ K2tog

◺ ssk

Chart 2

18

10

1

32-st rep

Stitch Key

☐ Knit

— Purl

◯ Yo

◿ K2tog

◺ ssk

⋀ SK2P

EDGING

Latvian (Two-Color) Cast-On

With A and B held tog, loosely tie a slipknot approx 6"/15cm from end. Place on larger needle and with B over thumb and A over index finger, cast on 80 sts (excluding slipknot) using long tail cast-on (see page 25). Divide sts evenly over two circular needles. Turn work so straight line of B is to the back and bumpy side of cast-on is facing you. Join, taking care not to twist sts. Place marker for end of rnd and sl marker every rnd.

Scallop

With A, work 4 rnds of Chart 1—64 sts.

CUFF

With B, k 1 rnd, p 1 rnd. With A, k 1 rnd, p 1 rnd. With B, work 18 rnds of Chart 2, k 1 rnd. With A, k 1 rnd, p 1 rnd. With B, k 1 rnd, p 1 rnd. With A, k 1 rnd.

LEG

Work 12 rnds of Chart 3 three times, then rnds 1–11 once.

HEEL

Redistribute sts on needles as foll: With Needle 1, k across then cont to k5 from Needle 2; with Needle 2, cont in pat to end then work 8 sts in pat from Needle 1—29 sts on Needle 1 (sole), 35 sts on Needle 2 (instep).

Heel flap

Worked only on 29 sts of Needle 1.

Row 1 K1 tbl, k27, sl 1 wyif, turn.

Row 2 K1 tbl, *p1, sl 1; rep from *, end sl 1 wyif.

Rep rows 1 and 2 eleven times.

Turn heel

Row 1 K1 tbl, k16, k2tog, k1, turn.

Row 2 Sl 1, p4, p2tog, p1, turn.

Row 3 Sl 1, k to 1 st before gap, k2tog tbl, k1, turn.

Row 4 Sl 1, p to 1 st before gap, p2tog, p1, turn.

Rep rows 3 and 4 until all heel sts have been worked—17 sts.

GUSSETS

Rnd 1 For Needle 1, sl 1, k16, pick up and k15 along side of heel flap; for Needle 2, pick up and k 1 st tbl at beg of instep, work across instep sts in pat (Row 1 of Chart 4), pick up and k 1 st tbl at end of instep.

Rnd 2 For Needle 1, pick up and k15 sts along side of heel flap, k29, k2tog, k1; for Needle 2, k2tog, pat to last 2 sts, ssk—81 sts.

Rnd 3 For Needle 1, k1, ssk, k to last 3 sts, k2tog, k1; for Needle 2, work even in pat as est.

Rnd 4 Knit.

Rep rnds 3 and 4 until 65 sts rem, then rep rnds 3 and 4 once EXCEPT working only first dec at beg of rnd 3—64 sts.

Chart 3

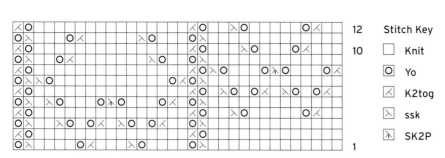

12

10

1

32-st rep

Stitch Key

☐ Knit

Ⓞ Yo

◿ K2tog

◺ ssk

⟑ SK2P

Chart 4

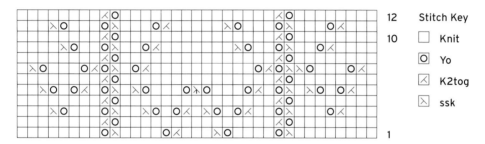

12

10

1

35-st rep

Stitch Key

☐ Knit

Ⓞ Yo

◿ K2tog

◺ ssk

Chart 5

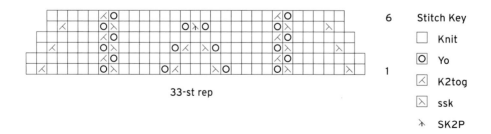

6

1

33-st rep

Stitch Key

☐ Knit

Ⓞ Yo

◿ K2tog

◺ ssk

⟑ SK2P

FOOT

Work in St st on Needle 1 and Chart 4 on Needle 2 until foot measures 7¼"/18.5cm or 2"/5cm less than desired length, ending with rnd 12.

TOE

Rnd 1 For Needle 1, work even in St st; for Needle 2, work Chart 5.

Rnd 2 Knit.

Rnds 3, 4, 5 and 6 Rep rnds 1 and 2—58 sts.

Rnd 7 *For Needle 1, k1, ssk, k to last 3 sts, k2tog, k1; rep from * for Needle 2.

Rnd 8 Knit.

Rep rnds 7 and 8 until 46 sts rem, then rep rnd 7 until 18 sts rem. Graft toe sts using Kitchener st (see Chapter 2).

FINISHED MEASUREMENTS

9"/23cm from cuff to heel

Approx 8"/20.5cm from heel to toe

MATERIALS

1 4oz/113g (560yd/512m) skein or ball of Schaefer Yarn Company **Anne** (wool/mohair/nylon) in light khaki mix

One set (5) dpns size 0 (2mm) OR SIZE TO OBTAIN GAUGE

GAUGE

36 sts and 48 rnds = 4"/10cm over St st using size 0 (2mm) dpn.

TAKE TIME TO CHECK GAUGE.

STITCH GLOSSARY

RT (Right Twist) K2 tog but do not drop from needle, k first st again, slip both sts off needle.

LT (Left Twist) Skip first st and k into back of 2nd st, k into first st, slip both sts off needle.

Estonian Socks

by Nancy Bush

Knit from the cuff down, these socks have a scalloped-edge cuff, a mini diamond cable pattern at the top and instep and a slip stitch pattern at the heel.

LEG

Cast on 80 sts. Divide sts over 4 needles as foll: 18 sts on Needle 1; 24 sts on Needle 2; 18 sts on Needle 3; 20 sts on Needle 4. Needles 1 and 2 hold the heel sts and Needles 3 and 4 hold the instep sts. Join, being careful not to twist sts. Place marker for end of rnd and sl marker every rnd.

Scalloped edge (chart 1)

Rnd 1 Knit.

Rnd 2 Purl.

Rnd 3 Knit.

Rnd 4 *K1, yo, k3, SK2P, k3, yo; rep from * around.

Rnd 5 Knit.

Rnds 6–13 Rep rnds 4 and 5 four times.

Rnd 14 Purl.

Leg pattern

Starting with rnd 1, work Chart 2 over Needles 1 and 2, work Chart 3 over Needles 3 and 4, inc 1 st at beg of Needle 3 on the first rnd—19 sts on Needle 3, 81 sts total. Work in chart pats until cuff measures 4"/10cm and rnd 5 of Chart 2 and rnd 21 of Chart 3 have been completed.

Next rnd P across Needles 1 and 2, inc 1 st at beg of Needle 1, and work rnd 10 of Chart 3 on Needles

Chart 1

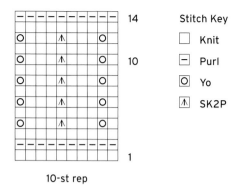

14

10

1

10-st rep

Stitch Key

☐ Knit

☐ Purl

☐ Yo

⋀ SK2P

Chart 2

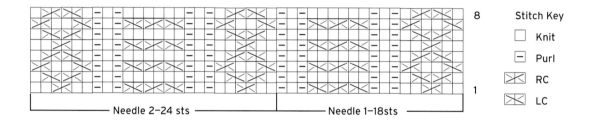

8

1

— Needle 2–24 sts — — Needle 1–18sts —

Stitch Key

☐ Knit

☐ Purl

☒ RC

☒ LC

Chart 3

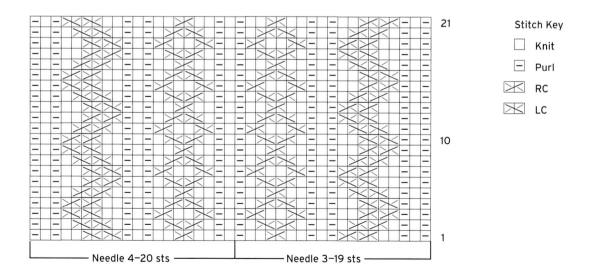

21

10

1

— Needle 4–20 sts — — Needle 3–19 sts —

Stitch Key

☐ Knit

☐ Purl

☒ RC

☒ LC

3 and 4—19 sts on Needle 1, 82 sts.

Cont working in St st on 43 back of leg sts and foll Chart 3 for front of leg until you have completed rnd 20 of Chart 3.

Leg shaping

Dec rnd At beg of Needle 1, ssk, k to last 2 sts of Needle 2, k2tog; work rnd 21 of instep chart. Rep dec rnd every 12 rnds 3 times more, which will coincide with rnd 21 of Chart 3—74 sts. Work even in patterns as established until leg measures 9"/23cm or desired length to top of heel flap.

HEEL

Sl 20 sts of Needle 2 onto Needle 1—35 sts on one needle. Heel flap is worked back and forth over these sts.

Row 1 *Sl 1, k1; rep from *, end k1, turn.

Row 2 Sl 1, p34.

Row 3 Sl 1, *sl 1, k1; rep from * to end.

Row 4 Rep row 2.

Rep rows 1-4 until there are 32 rows in heel flap.

Turn heel

Row 1 (RS) Sl 1, k17, skp, k1, turn.

Row 2 Sl 1, p2, p2tog, p1, turn.

Row 3 Sl 1, k to 1 st before gap, skp, k1, turn.

Row 4 Sl 1, p to 1 st before gap, p2tog, p1, turn.

Rep rows 3 and 4 until all sts have been worked —19 sts.

GUSSETS

With spare dpn, k10; with Needle 1, k9, pick up and k16 sts along side of heel flap, with Needles 2 and 3, work across 39 instep sts in pat as established (rnd 10 of instep pat); with Needle 4, pick up and k16 sts along side of heel flap and k10 sts from spare dpn—90 sts, 25 sts on Needle 1, 39 instep sts divided onto Needles 2 and 3, and 26 sts on Needle 4. Place marker for end of rnd.

Shape gussets

Rnd 1 For Needle 1, k to last 3 sts, k2tog, k1; for Needles 2 and 3, work in pat as established; for Needle 4, k1, ssk, k to end.

Rnd 2 For Needles 1 and 4, knit; for Needles 2 and 3, work in pat as established.

Rep rnds 1 and 2 until there are 72 sts.

Cont even in pats as established until 7 pattern reps have been work down the foot or until foot measures 2¾"/7cm less than desired length of foot, end with rnd 21 of instep.

TOE

Rnds 1-5 Knit.

Rnd 6 *K6, k2tog; rep from * around—63 sts.

Rnds 7-12 Knit.

Rnd 13 *K5, k2tog; rep from * around—54 sts.

Rnds 14-18 Knit.

Rnd 19 *K4, k2tog; rep from * around—45 sts.

Rnds 20-23 Knit.

Rnd 24 *K3, k2tog; rep from * around— 36 sts.

Rnds 25-27 Knit.

Rnd 28 *K2, k2tog; rep from * around—27 sts.

Rnds 29-30 Knit.

Rnd 30 *K1, k2tog; rep from * around—18 sts.

Rnd 31 Knit.

Rnd 32 *K2tog; rep from * around—9 sts.

Break yarn and thread through these live sts, pull up tightly to close toe and sew securely. Weave in ends and block socks under a damp towel or on sock blockers.

FINISHED MEASUREMENTS

7"/17.5cm from cuff to heel

Approx 7"/17.5cm from heel to toe

MATERIALS

2 1¾oz/50g skeins (each approx 222yd/203m of Brown Sheep Company **Cotton Fine** (cotton/wool) in #CF-005 cavern (A) and #CF-201 barn red (B)

1 skein in #CF-105 putty (C)

One set (5) dpns size 1 (2.25 mm) OR SIZE TO OBTAIN GAUGE

GAUGE

40 sts and 48 rnds = 4"/10cm over St st using size 1 (2.25mm) dpn.

TAKE TIME TO CHECK GAUGE.

Scandinavian Socks

By Priscilla Gibson-Roberts

These socks are knit from the toe up, with striped toes, heels and cuffs and graphic Scandinavian motifs. You can knit two slightly different socks, as shown, or a matching pair.

TOE

Notes Toe and heel are worked on two needles over one-half of the sts. One-half of the toe/heel is worked first, then the second half is worked and joined to the first half simultaneously. See Color Wheel socks on page 148 for instructions on working yos at the beginning of the row.

Using provisional crochet cast-on (see page 27) and A, cast on 37 sts.

Row 1 (WS) With A, p36, turn.

Row 2 Yo, [k1A, k1B] 17 times, k1A, turn.

Row 3 Yo, keeping in striped color pat as established, p to 1 st before last yo, turn.

Row 4 Yo, keeping in stripes as established, k to 1 st before last yo, turn.

Rep rows 3 and 4 until there are 19 sts between yos (last one on RH needle after turn) and 9 yos at each end.

Next row (RS) Keeping in stripes as established, k to next yo, sl yo to RH needle then sl back onto LH needle so leading side of loop is at front of needle, k2tog (working yo tog with next st), turn.

Next row Yo, keeping in stripes as established, p to next yo, [sl 1 knitwise, pick up loop at beg of row below, sl yo knitwise and p these 3 sts tog tbl], turn.

Chart 1

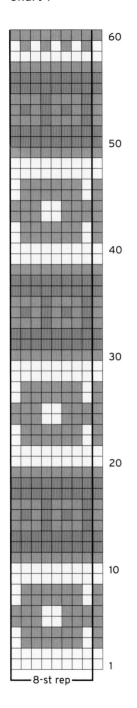

60

50

40

30

20

10

1

⌞ 8-st rep ⌟

Chart 2

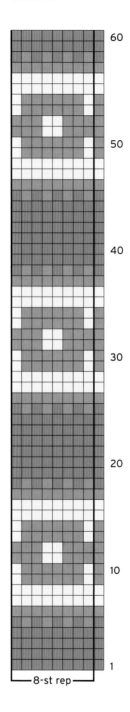

60

50

40

30

20

10

1

⌞ 8-st rep ⌟

Stitch Key

 Cavern (A)

Barn red (B)

☐ Putty (C)

Next row Yo, keeping in stripes as established, k to next yo, [sl yo to RH needle] twice, then sl both sts back onto LH needle so leading edge of loops is at front of needle, k3tog (working yos tog with next st), turn.

Next row Yo, keeping in stripes as established, p to next yo, sssp, turn.

Rep last 2 rows until there are 2 yos at each end. Drop B and rep last 2 rows in A. When there is one yo at each end, end in the middle of a RS row. Mark this center st for end of rnd—37 sts and 2 yos for sole.

FOOT

Remove waste yarn and place 36 sts onto 2 dpns for instep—73 sts and 2 yos. With B, k to next yo, k2tog (working yo tog with first instep st), then k to last stitch of instep and ssk tog with yo on next needle—73 sts.

Beg with st 1 of Chart 1, work 8-st rep 9 times for 60 rnds, or until foot measures 2"/5cm less than desired length to heel.

HEEL

With A, k37 sole sts, turn. Work same as toe, starting with row 1. Extend the length of the heel by working until there are 17 sts between yos and 10 yos at each end. Mark center st at back of heel for end of rnd.

LEG

Work 60 rnds of Chart 1, keeping to pat as established on foot, then k 2 rnds A, inc 4 sts on the first rnd. Work a band of vertical stripes (k1B, k1A) for 16 rnds. Finish band with k 5 rnds A, then bind off. Work all ends in, except the A and B at the top of the leg; with these 2 ends, make a twisted cord (see page 172), knot at end of a short length and trim rem yarn about 1"/2.5cm from knot.

For second sock substitute Chart 2 for Chart 1.

FINISHED MEASUREMENTS

4¼"/11cm from cuff to heel

Approx 9½"/24cm from heel to toe

MATERIALS

1 1¾ oz/50g ball each (approx 191yd/175m) Dale of Norway **Baby Ull** (wool) in #3871 brown (A), #2232 camel (B), #9436 moss green (C), #7854 dark green (D), #2015 yellow (E), #4227 red (F) and #5711 grey (G)

One set (4) dpns size 3 (3.25mm) OR SIZE TO OBTAIN GAUGE

One pair size 3 (3.25mm) needles

GAUGE

30 sts and 28 rnds = 4"/10cm over St st foll chart using size 3 (3.25mm) needles.

TAKE TIME TO CHECK GAUGE.

Turkish Socks

by Mari Lynn Patrick

These socks integrate traditional Turkish motifs and color patterns in a Western top-down sock design with a heel flap, gusset and wedge toes.

CUFF

With straight needles and A, cast on 60 sts. K 2 rows. With F, p 1 row, k 1 row. Divide sts evenly over 3 needles. Join, taking care not to twist sts. Place marker for end of rnd and sl marker every rnd.

LEG

Work 7 rnds of Chart 1.

Work 2 rnds of Chart 2, inc 3 sts evenly across rnd 2—63 sts.

Work 20 rnds of Chart 3. Break off yarns.

HEEL

Heel flap is worked back and forth over 30 sts. Sl the first 15 sts of Needle 1 and the last 15 sts of Needle 3 onto one needle—30 sts. Divide rem 33 sts onto 2 needles for instep to be worked later.

Work 2 rows of Chart 1 once, then work 2 rows of Chart 4 six times. Heel flap should measure approx 2"/5cm.

Turn heel

Next row (RS) K17, k2tog, k1, turn.

Row 2 Sl 1, p5, p2tog, p1, turn.

Row 3 Sl 1, k to 1 st before gap, k2tog, k1, turn.

Row 4 Sl 1, p to 1 st before gap, p2tog, p1, turn.

Chart 1

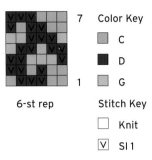

7

1

6-st rep

Color Key

- C
- D
- G

Stitch Key

- ☐ Knit
- Ⅴ Sl 1

Chart 2

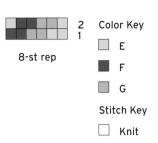

2
1

8-st rep

Color Key

- E
- F
- G

Stitch Key

- ☐ Knit

Chart 3

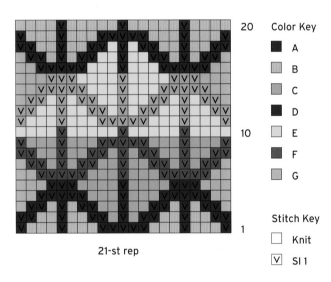

20

10

1

21-st rep

Color Key

- A
- B
- C
- D
- E
- F
- G

Stitch Key

- ☐ Knit
- Ⅴ Sl 1

Chart 4

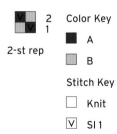

2
1

2-st rep

Color Key

- A
- B

Stitch Key

- ☐ Knit
- Ⅴ Sl 1

Rep rows 3 and 4 until all sts have been worked—18 sts.

Gussets

Note When working first 2 gusset rows, work 2 rnds of Chart 2. For tweed sock, work Chart 4 or for color pat sock, alternate Chart 3 and Chart 4.

With spare needle, k9; with Needle 1, k9, pick up and k16 sts along side of heel flap; with Needle 2, work across 33 instep sts; with Needle 3, pick up and k16 sts along side of heel flap, k9 from spare needle—83 sts. Place marker for end of rnd and redistribute sts as foll: 24 sts on Needle 1, 36 sts on Needle 2 (instep) and 23 sts on Needle 3.

Shape gussets

Rnd 1 Knit.

Rnd 2 For Needle 1, K to last 2 sts, k2tog; for Needle 2, k to end; for Needle 3, skp, k to end.

Rep rnds 1 and 2 until there are 63 sts.

FOOT

Cont in chosen pat until foot measures 8"/20.5cm or 2"/5cm less than desired length. For tweed pat sock, end last 2 rnds.

TOE

Redistribute sts as foll: 16 sts on Needle 1, 31 sts on Needle 2 and 16 sts on Needle 3.

Note Work chart 4 only while shaping toe.

Rnd 1 For Needle 1 K to last 3 sts, k2tog, k1; for Needle 2, k1, skp, k to last 3 sts, k2tog, k1; for Needle 3, k1, skp, k to end.

Rnd 2 Knit.

Rep rnds 1 and 2 until there are 25 sts. With Needle 3, k6 from Needle 1. With A, close toe using Kitchener st (see chapter 2).

FINISHING

Block socks. Sew cuff seam.

FINISHED MEASUREMENTS

7½"/19cm from cuff to heel

Approx 10"/25.5cm from heel to toe

MATERIALS

1 1¾ oz/50g skein (approx 222yd/203m) Brown Sheep Company **Cotton Fine** (cotton/wool) each in #CF-005 cavern (CC), #CF-100 cotton ball (MC), #CF-201 barn red (A), #CT-560 my blue heaven (B), #CF-345 gold dust (C), #CF-710 prosperous plum (D), #CF-310 wild orange (E) and #CF-470 holly green (F)

One set (5) dpns sizes 0 and 1 (2mm and 2.25mm) OR SIZE TO OBTAIN GAUGE

GAUGE

38 sts and 42 rnds = 4"/10cm over chart pat in St st using size 1 (2.25mm) needles.

TAKE TIME TO CHECK GAUGE.

Color Wheel Socks

by Priscilla Gibson-Roberts

This sock is knit from the toe up with a short-row toe and heel worked in intarsia and the cuff worked in two-color knitting.

SOCK

TOE

With smaller needle and provisional crochet cast-on (see page 27), cast on 42 sts. Work Toe Chart as foll:

Row 1 (WS) Purl, turn.

Row 2 K to last st, turn.

Row 3 Yo, p to last st, turn.

Row 4 Yo, k to 1 st before last yo, turn.

Row 5 Yo, p to 1 st before last yo, turn.

Rep rows 4 and 5 until there are 15 sts between yos (last one on RH needle after turn).

Next row (RS) Yo, k to next yo, sl yo to RH needle then sl back onto LH needle so leading side of loop is at front of needle, k2tog, turn.

Next row Yo, p to next yo, SSP, turn.

Next row Yo, k to next yo, [sl yo to RH needle] twice then sl both sts back onto LH needle so leading edge of loop is at front of needle, k3tog, turn.

Next row Yo, p to next yo, SSSP, turn.

Rep last 2 rows until all yos have been worked, end in the middle of a RS row. Break off yarn.

FOOT

Remove waste yarn and place 42 sts onto 2 dpns—84 sts. Change to larger needles. Beg

Toe Chart

Stitch Key

- ⊙ Yo
- ⊼ K2tog on RS, p2tog on WS
- ⋌ Ssk on RS, ssp on WS
- ⊼ K3tog on RS, p3tog on WS
- ⋌ Sssk on RS, sssp on WS

Color Key

- ■ A
- ■ B
- □ C

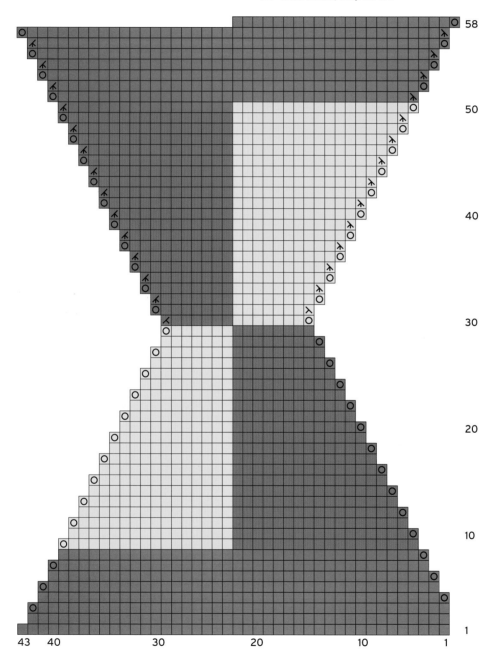

Foot Chart

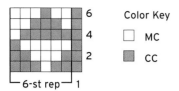

6
4
2
6-st rep 1

Color Key

☐ MC
▨ CC

Leg Chart

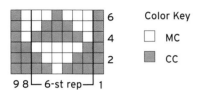

6
4
2
9 8 6-st rep 1

Color Key

☐ MC
▨ CC

Cuff Chart

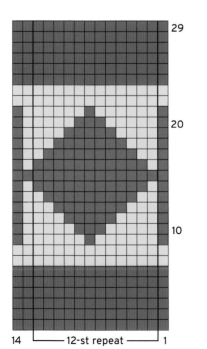

29

20

10

14 12-st repeat 1

Color Key

■ A
■ B
☐ C

with st 1 of Foot Chart at center back, work 6-st rep 13 times then sts 2–6 for 54 rnds or until foot measures 2 ¼"/5.5cm less than desired length. Work first 21 sts of next rnd, turn.

HEEL

Change to smaller needles and work same as toe, starting with row 1 across 42 sts of sole. Inc 3 sts on last WS row across back of heel—87 sts.

LEG

Change to larger needles. Beg with st 1 at center back of Leg Chart, work 6-st rep 14 times then sts 8–9 for 54 rnds or until leg measures 2 ½"/6.5cm less than desired length.

CUFF

Beg with st 1 of Cuff Chart, work 12-st rep 7 times then sts 14-15 for 29 rnds. P 1 rnd, k 5 rnds. Fold hem to inside at purl ridge and hem stitch in place.

Second sock

Work same as first sock with colors D, E and F.

FINISHED MEASUREMENTS

13.5"/34.5cm from cuff to heel

Approx 7.5"/19cm from beginning of the arch shaping to toe

MATERIALS

1 3½oz/100g skein (approx 360yd/329m) Schoolhouse Press **Satakieli** (wool) each in #894 hunter green (A) and #3 cream (B)

One set (5) dpns size 3 (3.25mm) OR SIZE TO OBTAIN GAUGE

GAUGE

28 sts and 28 rnds = 4"/10cm over chart pat using size 3 (3.25mm) needles.

TAKE TIME TO CHECK GAUGE.

Arched Shaped Socks

by Meg Swansen

"This design was found in stockings knit for me by Elizabeth Zimmermann in the 1960s. It had never been published, and I couldn't find any notes in EZ's journals. A careful dissection of the original revealed a sculptural construction with a very sensuous fitted arch under the foot. A good type of increase for the actual arch shaping is knit-into-the-back-of-the-stitch-of-the-row-below in a mirror-image on each side of the central stitch(es) of the underfoot."

LEG

With A, cast on 80 sts. Divide sts evenly over 4 needles. Join, taking care not to twist sts. Place marker for end of rnd and sl marker every rnd. Work 1 rnd in k1, p1 rib.

Next rnd *P1 A, k1 B; rep from * around.

Rep this rnd 5 times more, redistributing sts on needles as foll: 23 sts on Needle 1; 17 sts on Needle 2; 23 sts on Needle 3; 17 sts on Needle 4.

Begin chart

Next rnd Needle 1: *K1 A, k1 B; rep from * to end of needle; Needle 2: work rnd 1 of chart pat to end of needle; Needle 3: *k1 A, k1 B; rep from * to end of needle; Needle 4: work rnd 1 of chart pat to end of needle.

Work rnds 1–24 of chart once, then cont to rep rnds 5–24 for pat. Cont in pats as established until piece measures 6.5"/16.5cm from beg.

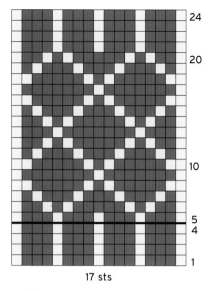

24

20

10

5
4

1

17 sts

Color Key

■ A

□ B

Dec rnd Needle 1: Ssk, work to last 2 sts, k2tog; Needle 2: work even; Needle 3: ssk, work to last 2 sts, k2tog; Needle 4: work even. Rep dec rnd every 7 rnds 5 times more = 56 ankle sts. Work even until piece measures 13.5"/34.5cm from beg, or desired length to heel.

HEEL

Heel flap

Next row (RS) With Needle 4, work 7 sts from Needle 1; with Needle 1, work rem 4 sts, 17 sts from Needle 2, and first 4 sts from Needle 3—25 sts on Needle 1; 31 instep sts on Needles 3 and 4. Work back and forth on 25 sts of Needle 1 only in pats as established for 3"/7.5cm.

Turn heel

Turn heel on 11 sts as follows:

Row 1 Work 18 sts, ssk, turn.

Row 2 Slip 1, work 9 sts, p2tog, turn.

Row 3 Sl 1, work 9 sts, ssk, turn.

Row 4 Slip 1, work 9 sts, p2tog, turn.

Rep rows 3 and 4 until all 7 sts on both sides of center 11 sts have been worked—11 sts rem.

Next rnd (RS) With 11 sts on needle, pick up and k15 sts along side of heel flap, work across the 31 instep sts and pick up and k15 sts along other side of heel flap—72 sts. Redistribute sts over 4 needles.

Note: Keep center 17 sts of instep in chart pat and rem sts in 2-color pat up to the toe shaping.

Dec rnd Work to the last 2 picked up sts at side of heel, *k2tog, work across instep sts, ssk, work to end of rnd.

Next rnd Work even.

Rep last 2 rnds until there are 58 sts, AT THE SAME TIME, about 5 rnds after heel turn, at the underfoot, establish arch shaping as foll: Mark center st of heel.

Next rnd Work to 5 sts before marked st, k2tog, place marker, work 3 sts, M1, k1 (center st), M1, work 3 sts, place marker, ssk, work to end of rnd.

Next rnd Work even.

Shaping rnd Work to 2 sts before first dec marker, k2tog, slip marker, work to center st, M1, k1, M1, work to second dec marker, slip marker, ssk, work to end of rnd.

Rep these 2 rnds 11 times more, then work even until 2"/5cm less than desired foot length if necessary.

TOE

Place a marker each side of 17-st Center Chart Pat.

Next rnd Work to 3 sts before marker, k2tog, k1 A, [k1 B, k1 A] 9 times, ssk, work to end of rnd.

Rep last rnd until 20 sts rem. Weave sts tog using Kitchener st (see Chapter 2).

FINISHED MEASUREMENTS

9 ¼"/23.5cm from cuff to heel

Approx 11 ½"/29cm from heel to toe

MATERIALS

2 1¾ oz/50g skeins (each approx 181yd/166m) Lana Gatto/Needful Yarns, Inc. **Wool Gatto** (wool) in #5000 black (A)

1 skein each #8000 white (B), and #2536 turquoise (C).

One set (4) dpns size 3 (3.25mm) OR SIZE TO OBTAIN GAUGE

One pair each sizes 2 and 3 (2.75 and 3.25mm) needles

GAUGE

28 sts and 36 rnds = 4"/10cm over St st using size 3 (3.25mm) needles.

TAKE TIME TO CHECK GAUGE.

Man's Classic Argyles

by Shirley Paden

This sock is knit flat from cuff to heel, then joined for working in the round from the ankle with heel flap and wedge toe. Seams are at insides of legs.

CUFF

With smaller straight needles and A, cast on 62 sts.

Row 1 K1 (selvage st), *k2, p2; rep from *, end k1 (selvage st).

Row 2 P1, *p2, k2; rep from *, end p1.

Rep rows 1 and 2 for 2"/5cm. Change to larger straight needles.

LEG

Keeping first and last sts in St st for selvage, work 58 rows of chart, dec 1 selvage st each side on last RS row—60 sts. Break off yarn.

HEEL

Heel flap

Heel flap is worked back and forth over 30 sts only—first 30 sts of leg for right sock and last 30 sts for left sock (see chart). Sl rem 30 sts onto 2 dpns for instep to be worked later. With RS facing, join A where noted on chart for beg of heel flap.

Row 1 (RS) *Sl 1, k1; rep from * to end.

Row 2 Sl 1, p to end.

Rep rows 1 and 2 until there are 34 rows in heel flap.

Beg left
sock heel

Beg right
sock heel

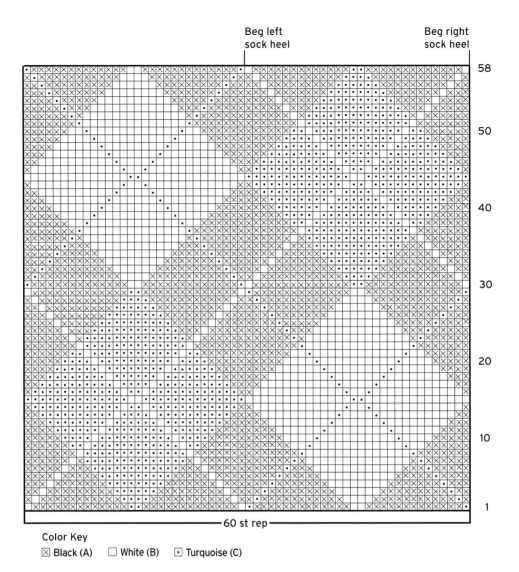

58

50

40

30

20

10

1

◀— 60 st rep —▶

Color Key

⊠ Black (A)   ☐ White (B)   ⊡ Turquoise (C)

Turn heel

Row 1 (RS) K17, ssk, k1, turn.

Row 2 Sl 1, p5, p2tog, p1, turn.

Row 3 Sl 1, k to 1 st before gap, ssk, k1, turn.

Row 4 Sl 1, p to 1 st before gap, p2tog, p1, turn.

Rep rows 3 and 4 until all heel sts have been worked—18 sts.

GUSSETS

With RS facing and spare dpn, k9. With Needle 1, k9, pick up and k18 along side of heel flap. With Needle 2, k30 (instep sts). With Needle 3, pick up and k18 along side of heel flap, k9 from spare dpn—84 sts. Pm for end of rnd.

Gusset shaping

Rnd 1 Knit.

Rnd 2 For Needle 1, k to last 3 sts, k2tog, k1.

For Needle 2, knit. For Needle 3, k1, ssk, k to end.

Rep rnds 1 and 2 until there are 60 sts.

FOOT

Work even in St st until foot measures 8½"/21.5cm or 2"/5cm less than desired length.

TOE

Rnd 1 Knit.

Rnd 2 *For Needle 1, k to last 3 sts, k2tog, k1. For Needle 2, k1, ssk, k to last 3 sts, k2tog, k1, For Needle 3, k1, ssk, k to end.

Rep rnds 1 and 2 until there are 16 sts. With Needle 3, k4 from Needle 1. Graft toe sts using Kitchener st (see Chapter 2). Sew leg seam.

Embroidered Stockings

by Joan McGowan-Michael

These Victorian-inspired stockings are knit

from the toe up with shaping at the calf. Then

fanciful embroidered floral motifs are added.

FINISHED MEASUREMENTS

From bottom of heel to top of stocking, 18"/46cm unstretched

Will stretch to fit 26–30"/66–76cm length measured from bottom of heel, and all shoe sizes

MATERIALS

3 1½oz/50g balls (each approx 100yd/91m) of Cascade Yarns **Fixation** (cotton/elastic) in #8990 black

6 skeins (each approx 9yd/8m) of DMC Six-Strand Embroidery Floss (cotton) in #498 red

2 skeins in #309 light red

1 skein in #783 golden yellow

One set (5) dpns sizes 3 and 6 (3.25 and 4mm) OR SIZE TO OBTAIN GAUGE

Waste yarn, tapestry needle and 1yd/1m ¼"/.5cm black elastic

GAUGE

28 sts and 36 rnds = 4"/10cm over St st using smaller needles

24 sts and 32 rnds = 4"/10cm over St st using larger needles

TAKE TIME TO CHECK GAUGES.

Note

Yarn substitution is not recommended for this style, as the elastic and cotton combination in this yarn is an integral part of the design and fit.

TOE

Using provisional crochet cast-on (see page 27) with smaller needles, cast on 26 sts.

Row 1 (WS) Purl.

Row 2 K1, SKP, k to last 3 sts, k2tog, k1.

Rep rows 1 and 2 until 8 sts rem.

Next row Purl.

Next row Pick up and k1 from end of previous RS row on first half of toe, k to end, pick up and k1 from first half of toe as before.

Rep last 2 rows 8 times more—26 sts.

FOOT

Carefully remove waste yarn and slip 26 sts evenly over 2 dpns, divide rem 26 sts over 2 dpns—54 sts. K26 sole sts, pm for end of rnd. Work in St st until foot measures 6"/15cm or 2" less than desired length.

HEEL

Work back and forth as for toe starting with Row 1 over 26 sts of sole.

On last row of heel work across 13 sts, place end of rnd marker at center back heel, work 13 sts.

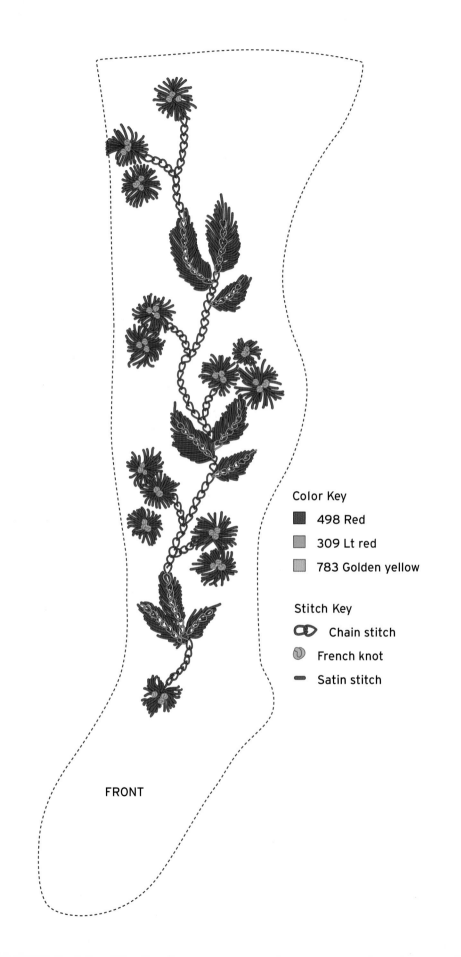

Color Key

■ 498 Red

■ 309 Lt red

□ 783 Golden yellow

Stitch Key

⬭ Chain stitch

𝆕 French knot

▬ Satin stitch

FRONT

Top

LEG

Cont working in the rnd on 4 needles until leg measures 4"/10cm from top of heel. Change to larger needles.

K 1 rnd.

Inc rnd K1, m1, k to last st, m1, k1—54 sts.

Rep last 2 rnds until there are 68 sts. Work even for 2½"/6.5cm.

Knit 3 rnds.

Dec rnd K1, ssk, k to last 3 sts, k2tog, k1.

Rep last 4 rnds until there are 62 sts.

Work even for 2½"/6.5cm, then work inc rnd every fourth rnd until there are 78 sts.

Work even for 2"/5cm or desired length to top of stocking.

Eyelet rnd *Yo, k2tog; rep from * around.

Bind off.

FINISHING

Cut elastic to fit and insert through eyelets at top of stocking. Sew ends of elastic together. With tapestry needle and embroidery floss, embroider stocking foll diagram (see photo for placement). Embroidery may be done up the sides of the legs and around the top.

Color Key

■ 498 Red

■ 309 Lt red

■ 783 Golden yellow

Stitch Key

⬭ Chain stitch

◔ French knot

━ Satin stitch

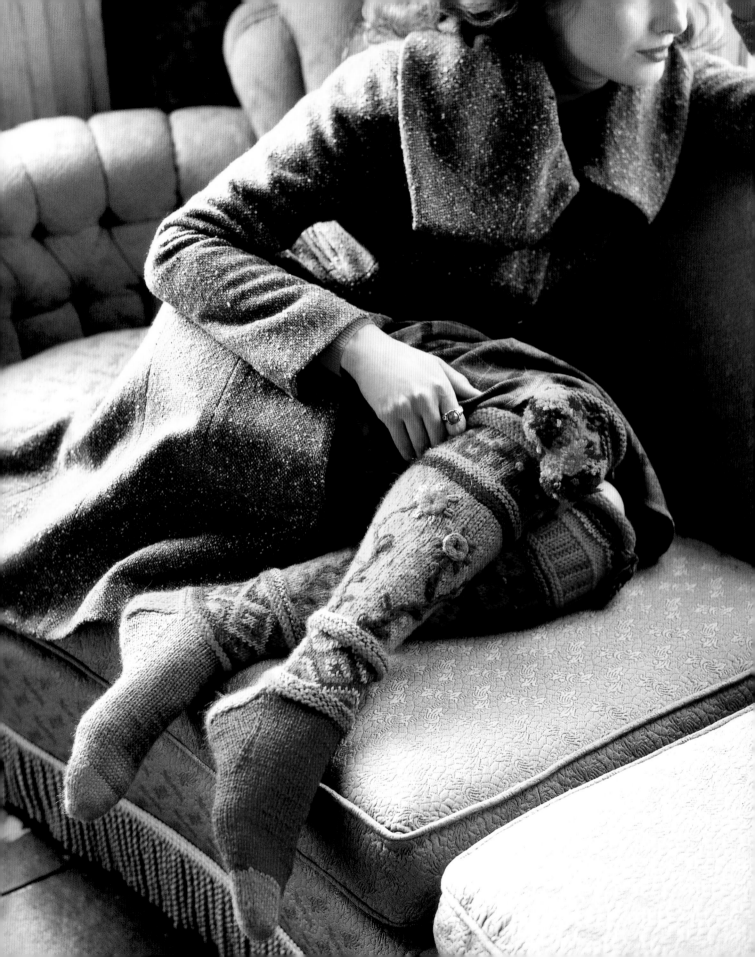

Embroidered Socks

by Kristin Nicholas

This sock is cast on at the ankle and knit up to the knee. This enables you to try on the sock and stop the increases for the calf once it fits you. Then you pick up stitches at the cast-on and work down to create a heel flap and foot with wedge toe.

FINISHED MEASUREMENTS

12"/30.5cm (14½"/37cm) calf circumference

20"/50.5cm from cuff to heel

Approx 9"/23cm from heel to toe

MATERIALS

2 1¾ oz/50g skeins each (approx 93yd/85m) Nashua Handknits/Westminster Fibers Inc. **Julia** (kid mohair/alpaca/wool) each in #4936 blue thyme (A), #3961 ladies mantle (B), and #3983 delphinium (C) 1 skein each in #8141 pretty pink (D), #2250 french pumpkin (E), #2083 magenta (F) and #2230 rock henna (G)

One set (5) dpns sizes 6 and 7 (4 and 4.5mm) OR SIZE TO OBTAIN GAUGE

Tapestry needle

GAUGE

20 sts and 26 rnds = 4"/10cm over St st using larger needles.

TAKE TIME TO CHECK GAUGE.

NOTE

Sock 1 colors are given first with Sock 2 colors in (parentheses) throughout. Directions are given for two sizes, with the larger size in (parentheses). If there is only one figure, it applies to both sizes. Smaller needles are used for the foot to give a snugger fit.

Ridge Pattern

Rnd 1 Knit.

Rnds 2 and 3 Purl.

Rep rnds 1–3.

LEG

Cast on 44 sts with larger dpns and F (E). Divide sts evenly over 4 needles. Join, taking care not to twist sts. Place marker for end of rnd and sl marker every rnd.

P 2 rnds.

Change to C (A) and work 3 rnds in ridge pat.

Work 13 rnds chart 1.

Change to F (D) and work 3 rnds in ridge pat.

Change to A (A) and work 3 rnds in ridge pat, inc 3 sts evenly around in first rnd—47 sts. Work chart 2 as foll: Work first 2 sts of chart, pm, work 4-st rep 11 times, pm, work last st of chart.

Inc rnd Pat to first marker, slip marker, m1, pat to next marker, m1, slip marker, pat to end, working incs into chart pats.

Rep inc rnd every third rnd until there are 60 (72) sts, working only first inc of last inc rnd. Remove inc markers, leaving end-of-rnd marker in place.

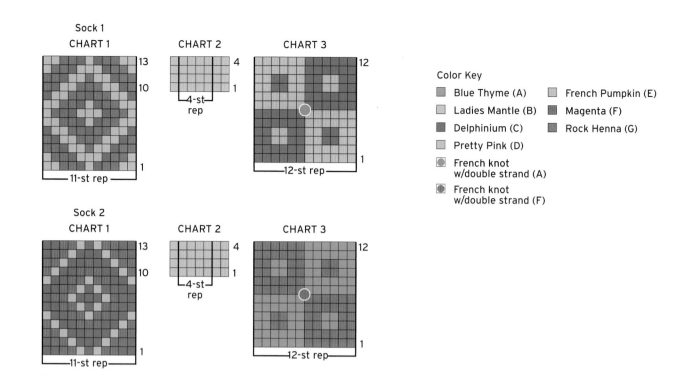

Sock 1

CHART 1

13

10

1

└─11-st rep─┘

CHART 2

4

1

└4-st┘
rep

CHART 3

12

1

└─12-st rep─┘

Sock 2

CHART 1

13

10

1

└─11-st rep─┘

CHART 2

4

1

└4-st┘
rep

CHART 3

12

1

└─12-st rep─┘

Color Key

■ Blue Thyme (A)
■ Ladies Mantle (B)
■ Delphinium (C)
■ Pretty Pink (D)
◉ French knot w/double strand (A)
◉ French knot w/double strand (F)

■ French Pumpkin (E)
■ Magenta (F)
■ Rock Henna (G)

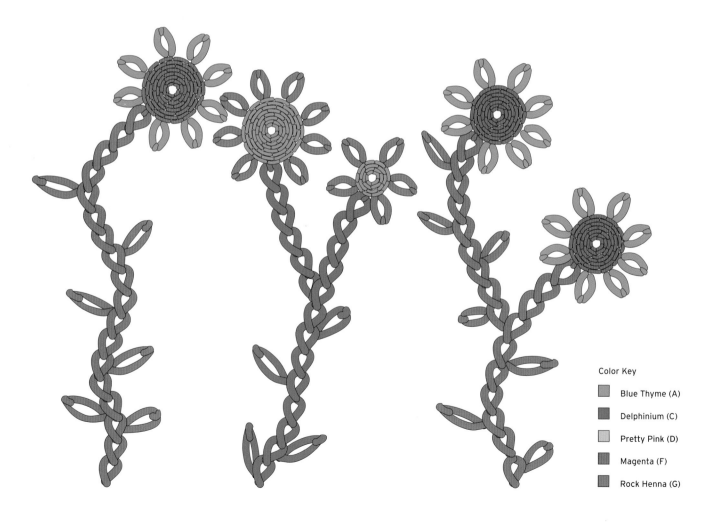

Color Key

■ Blue Thyme (A)
■ Delphinium (C)
■ Pretty Pink (D)
■ Magenta (F)
■ Rock Henna (G)

Work even in pat until piece measures 12"/30.5cm from beg or 8"/20.5cm less than desired length to top of cuff.

With A (C), work 3 rnds in ridge pat.

With G (B), work 3 rnds in ridge pat.

Work 12 rnds chart 3.

With A (F), work 3 rnds in ridge pat.

With F (E) work 3 rnds in ridge pat and dec as foll:

Large sock *K7, k2tog; rep from * around—64 sts.

Work in k2, p2 rib with F (E) for 1¼"/3cm.

CUFF

With F (E), p 1 rnd, k 3 rnds. This forms the turning ridge for cuff.

The sock is topped with a series of reverse St st ridges, but because the WS will be cuffed, the ridge pat is worked in reverse as foll:

Rnd 1 Purl.

Rnds 2 and 3 Knit.

Change to B (C) and purl next rnd.

Eyelet rnd K23 (29), k2tog, yo, k2, yo, k2tog, k23 (29).

K 1 rnd. Cont in ridge pat in reverse as foll: 3 rnds G (D), 3 rnds C (A), 3 rnds D (G), 3 rnds E (B).

Bind off knitwise with E (B). Return to cast-on edge to complete the sock.

HEEL

Heel flap

With E (D) and smaller dpn, pick up and k22

sts along cast-on edge—11 sts on each side of end of rnd. Make sure you have beg of rnd centered exactly on the 22 sts so the shaping and eyelets will fall in the correct spot on the leg. Work back and forth as foll:

Row 1 (WS) K1, p20, k1.

Row 2 K1, *k1, sl 1; rep from *, end k1.

Rep rows 1 and 2 until heel flap measures 2"/5cm, end with a RS row.

Turn heel

Row 1 (WS) P13, p2tog, p1, turn.

Row 2 Sl 1, k5, SKP, k1, turn.

Row 3 Sl 1, p to 1 st before gap, p2tog, p1, turn.

Row 4 Sl 1, k to 1 st before gap, SKP, k1, turn.

Rep rows 3 and 4 until all heel sts have been worked—14 sts.

GUSSETS

With A (C) and the needle the heel sts are on (Needle 1), pick up and k13 along side of heel flap—you'll be working toward the instep sts. With Needle 2, pick up and k22 from the cast-on edge. With Needle 3, pick up and k13 along other side of heel flap, k7 from Needle 1—2 sts. Place marker for end of rnd. K 1 rnd.

Gusset shaping

Rnd 1 For Needle 1, k to last 3 sts, k2tog, k1. For Needle 2, knit. For Needle 3, k1, SKP, k to end.

Rnd 2 Knit.

Rep rnds 1 and 2 until there are 44 sts.

FOOT

Work even in St st until foot measures 8"/20.5cm from back of heel or 2"/5cm from desired length.

TOE

Change to D (F).

Rnd 1 Knit.

Rnd 2 For Needle 1, k2tog, k1. For Needle 2, k1, SKP, k to last 3 sts, k2tog, k1. For Needle 3, k1, SKP, k to end.

Rep rnds 1 and 2 until there are 16 sts. With Needle 3, k4 from Needle 1. Graft toe sts using Kitchener st (see Chapter 2).

FINISHING

Embroidery

Embroider flowers in center of check pat section on leg foll diagram. With 2 strands A (F), make French knots (see Appendix) in the center row of chart 3 where the boxes join.

Tie

With 1 strand each D and C (D and B), chain approx 30"/76cm. Thread through the eyelets for tie.

Pompoms

Using 4 different colors, make four 1½–2"/4-5cm pompoms (see Appendix). Sew one to each end of tie.

Abbreviations

approx	approximate(ly)		pm	place marker
beg	beginning		Psso	pass slipped st over
cc	contrast color		oz	ounce(s)
cm	centimeter(s)		RC	right cross
cn	cable needle		rem	remain
cont	continue		rep	repeat
dec	decrease		RH	right hand
dpn(s)	double-pointed needle(s)		rnd(s)	round(s)
est	establish(ed)		RPC	right purl cross
foll	follow(ing)(s)		RPT	right purl twist
g	gram(s)		RS	right side
inc	increase		RT	right twist
k	knit		S2KP	(centered double dec) slip 2 tog knitwise, k1, p2sso
kfb	knit in front and back of			
LC	left cross		SK2P	(double dec) slip 1, k2tog, psso
LH	left hand		skp	slip, knit and pass
LPC	left purl cross		sl	slip
LPT	left purl twist		ssk	[slip 1 knitwise] twice, k2tog tbl
LT	left twist		ssp	[slip 1 knitwise] twice, p2tog tbl
m	meter(s)		sssp	[slip 1 knitwise] 3 times, p3tog tbl
M1	make 1		sssk	[slip 1 knitwise] 3 times, k3tog tbl
M1L	(Left slanting inc) With LH needle, lift strand between needles from front to back and k tbl.			
			st(s)	stitch(es)
M1R	(Right slanting inc) With LH needle, lift strand between needles from back to front and k.		St st	stockinette stitch
			tog	together
			WS	wrong side
MB	make bobble		WT	wrap & turn
MC	main color		WW	work wrap(s)
mm	millimeters		wyib	with yarn in back
p	purl		wyif	with yarn in front
pat(s)	pattern(s)		yd	yard(s)
pfb	purl in front and back of		yo	yarn over

Techniques

Slipknot

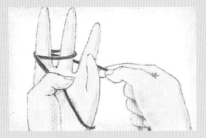

1 Hold the short end of the yarn in your palm with your thumb. Wrap the yarn twice around the index and middle fingers.

2 Pull the strand attached to the ball through the loop between your two fingers, forming a new loop.

3 Place the new loop on the needle. Tighten the loop on the needle by pulling on both ends of the yarn to form the slipknot. You are now ready to cast-on.

Single Cast-On

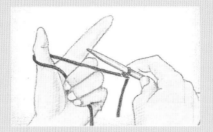

1 Place a slip knot on the right needle, leaving a short tail. Wrap the yarn from the ball around your left thumb from front to back and secure it in your palm with your other fingers.

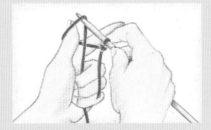

2 Insert the needle upward through the strand on your thumb.

3 Slip this loop from your thumb onto the needle, pulling the yarn from the ball to tighten it. Continue in this way until all the stitches are cast on.

Pompoms

You can use pompoms as a decorative trim, at the ends of cords, on hats or hoods, and for children's garments. They are easy to make.

1 With two circular pieces of cardboard the width of the desired pompom, cut a center hole. Then cut a pie-shaped wedge out of the circle.

2 Hold the two circles together and wrap the yarn tightly around the cardboard. Carefully cut around the cardboard.

3 Tie a piece of yarn tightly between the two circles. Remove the cardboard and trim the pompom.

Embroidery Stitches

Chain stitch **French knot** **Satin stitch**

I-Cord

I-cord is made on double-pointed needles. Cast on about three to five stitches. *Knit one row. Without turning the work, slip the stitches back to the beginning of the row. Pull the yarn tightly from the end of the row. Repeat from the * as desired. Bind off.

Twisted Cord

Twisted cord is made by twisting strands of yarn together. The thickness of the cord will depend on the number and weight of the strands. Cut strands three times the desired finished length and knot them about one inch (2.5cm) from each end.

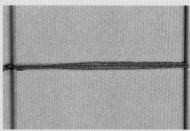

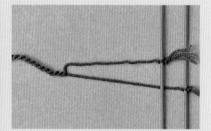

1 If you have someone to help you, insert a pencil or knitting needle through each end of the strands. If not, place one end over a doorknob and put a pencil through the other end. Turn the strands clockwise until they are tightly twisted.

2 Keeping the strands taut, fold the piece in half. Remove the pencils and allow the cords to twist onto themselves.

Vogue®Knitting Sock Worksheet

Date: _____

This pair of socks is for_____

Measurements:

        Ankle circumference:_____ Foot circumference:_____

        Length of foot: _____ Length of sock leg: _____

        Additional measurements:_____

Yarn:

        Manufacturer: _____ Yarn name:_____

        Color/dye lot: _____ Number of yards: _____

Stitch pattern name/source:_____

        Number of stitches in pattern repeat:_____

Needle size and type: _____

Gauge:

        In stockinette stitch:_____ In pattern: _____

Sock construction method:_____

        Heel shape: _____ Toe shape: _____

Number of stitches to cast on:_____

Notes and comments:_____

_____

_____

_____

Resources

Blue Moon Fiber Arts
56587 Mollenhour Road
Scappoose, OR 97056
www.bluemoonfiberarts.com

Brown Sheep Company
100662 County Road 16
Mitchell, NE 69357
www.brownsheep.com

Cascade Yarns
1224 Andover Parke E
Tukwila, WA 98188
www.cascadeyarns.com

Dale of Norway
4750 Shelburne Road
Shelburne, VT 05482
www.dale.no

Koigu Wool Designs
Box 158
563295 Glenelg Holland Townline
Chatsworth, Ontario NOH 1G0
Canada
www.koigu.com

Lana Gatto
distributed by Needful Yarns, Inc.

Lana Grossa
distributed by Unicorn Books & Crafts
1338 Ross Street
Petaluma, CA 94954
www.unicornbooks.com

Lorna's Laces
4229 North Honore Street
Chicago, IL 60613
www.lornaslaces.net

Louet Sales
808 Commerce Park Drive
Ogdensburg, NY 13669
In Canada:
R.R. 4
Prescott, Ontario KOE 1TO
Canada
www.louet.com

Nashua Handknits
distributed by Westminster Fibers, Inc.

Naturally NZ
15 Church Street
Onehunga
Auckland, New Zealand
www.naturallyyanrsnz.com
In the U.S.:
Fiber Trends
P.O. Box 7266
East Wenatchee, WA 98802
www.fibertrends.com
In Canada:
The Old Mill Knitting Company
P.O. Box 81176
Ancaster, Ontario L9G 4XZ
Canada

Needful Yarns, Inc.
60 Industrial Parkway PMB #233
Cheektowaga, NY 14227
In Canada:
4476 Chesswood Drive, Unit 10-11
Toronto, Ontario M3J 2B9
Canada
www.needfulyarnsinc.com

Schaefer Yarn Company
3514 Kelly's Corners Rd.
Interlaken, NY 14847
www.schaeferyarn.com

Schoeller & Stahl
distributed by Skacel Collection, Inc.

Schoolhouse Press
6899 Cary Bluff
Pittsville, WI 54466
www.schoolhousepress.com

Skacel Collection, Inc.
P.O. Box 88110
Seattle, WA 98138
www.skacelknitting.com

Westminster Fibers
4 Townsend Avenue, Unit 8
Nashua, NH 03063
www.westminsterfibers.com

Zitron
distributed by Skacel Collection, Inc.